بسم الله الرحمن الرحيم

In the name of Allah, All-Merciful and Compassionate

The World of the Angels

Shaykh 'Abdu'l-Hamid Kishk

Dar Al-Taqwa

© Dar Al Taqwa Ltd. 1994

Reprinted : June 1999 / Rabi Al-Awwal 1420

ISBN 1 870582 00 6

Translation: Aisha Bewley

Editorial: Abdalhaqq Bewley

Production: Bookwork, Slough.

Published by:
    Dar Al Taqwa Ltd.
    7A Melcombe Street
    Baker Street
    London NW1 6AE

Printed and bound in Great Britain by
DELUXE PRINTERS
245a Acton Lane,
London NW10 7NR.

Table of Contents

Preface   1

The Obligation of Belief in the Angels   3

The Creation of the Angels   5
The Wings of the Angels   6
The Magnitude of the Angels   6
The Beauty of the Angels   7
The Number of the Angels   8
The Worship and Glorification of the Angels   9
The Frequented House   9

The Story of Adam and the Angels   11
Adam's Greeting to the Angels   12

The Different Types of Angels   14
Jibril, Mika'il and Israfil   14
The Angel of Death   16
The Guardian Angels   17
The Recording Angels   18
Munkar and Nakir   20
The Custodians of the Garden and the Fire   21
Angels entrusted with the sperm in the womb   24
The Bearers of the Throne   25
The Karubiyyun   25
The Angel of the Mountains   26
The Angels of the Ranks   26
The Angels of *dhikr*   27
Angels of Visions   29

Different Forms in which the Angels appear 31
The Story of Maryam 32
Angels being sent to test mankind 34
The Angel of Death coming to Musa 35

The Story of Harut and Marut 37
The true interpretation of the *aya*t 41

Jibril: the Envoy to the Prophets 44
The Attributes of Jibril 48
The Enmity of the Jews to Jibril 50
The Night Journey of the Messenger of Allah 52
Jibril teaching the Prophet *Wudu'* and the Prayer 55
The Angels coining a Metaphor for the Prophet 56
Jibril giving good news of the Garden to Khadija 56
Jibril leading the Angels in the Battle of Badr 58
The Angels in the Battle of the Confederates 59
The Angels helping the Prophet against the Jews 62
The Angels in the Battle of Hunayn 63

An Extraordinary Dream 65

Righteous actions whose doers are prayed for by the Angels 71
Obedience to Allah on the Night of Power 71
Recitation of Qur'an and *dhikr* of Allah 72
Teaching People Good 75
The seeker of useful knowledge 76
Walking to the Mosque and Remaining there 77
Praying in the first row 78
Going early to *Jumu'a* 79
The *Fajr* and *'Asr* prayers in the mosque 80
The meal of *Sahur* 80
Sadaqa and spending in good ways 81
The *Hajj* and standing at 'Arafa 82
Seeking martyrdom in the way of Allah 83
The prayer on the Prophet 84
Visiting the Sick 84
Visiting Brothers 85

ii

Supplication for believers who are not present   85
Sleeping in a state of *wudu'*   86

Actions whose doers are cursed by the Angels   87
The curse on the unbelievers   87
Preventing the implementation of the *Shari'a*   87
Sheltering people of innovation   88
Abusing the Companions   88
Women not responding to their husbands   89
A woman going out without permission   90
Someone pointing at his brother with a weapon   90

The Believer's Obligation towards the Angels   92
Not spitting to the right during the Prayer   93

iii

Preface

Praise be to Allah. We praise Him, seek His help and ask His forgiveness. We seek refuge with Allah from the evils of ourselves and from our bad actions. Whoever Allah guides no one can lead astray. Whoever He leads astray, no one can guide. I testify that there is no god but Allah alone without any partner. The Kingdom is His and all praise is His and He is over all things powerful. I testify that Sayyiduna Muhammad is His slave and Messenger, His chosen one among His creation and His friend. He conveyed the message and handed over the trust and advised the Community. By means of him Allah removed sorrow and effaced the darkness. He strove in the way of Allah until the Certain came to him. May Allah repay you for us, O my master, O Messenger of Allah, in the best way that any Prophet can be repaid from his community and any Messenger from his people!

"O you who believe! Be fearful of Allah in the way he should be feared, and do not die except as submitted Muslims." (3:102)

"O People of mankind! Be fearful of your Lord, who created you from one self, and created from it its mate, and from the two of them has dispersed about many men and women. Be fearful of Allah, Him by Whom you make demands of one another, and about ties of kinship. Allah is watchful over you." (4:1)

"O you who believe! Be fearful of Allah and speak words which hit the mark. He will make your actions right for you and forgive you your wrong deeds. He who obeys

Allah and His Messenger has won a mighty victory."
(33:70-71)

My intention in this book is to present one of the pillars of belief in full detail. This pillar is belief in the angels. Allah Almighty says:

"The Messenger believes in what has been sent down to him from his Lord, and so do the believers. Each one believes in Allah and His angels and His Books and His Messengers. We do not differentiate between any of His Messengers. They say, "We hear and we obey. Forgive us, our Lord! To You is the journey's end." (2:283)

This firm pillar and sound foundation must be fully understood. Here we will give authority to the lights of revelation and be guided by them within this precious world, the world of the angels, in the name of which Allah has praised Himself. He says:

"Praise belongs to Allah, the Bringer-into-being of the heavens and the earth, the Maker of the angels into messengers, possessing wings - two, three and four. He adds to creation in any way He wills. Allah is over all things powerful." (35:1)

I ask Allah Almighty to grant the best of knowledge and sincere action to the reader of this book. He is Hearing, Near-at-Hand, and the Answerer of supplication.

Shaykh 'Abdu'l-Hamid Kishk

2

The Obligation of Belief in the Angels

Allah - glory be to Him and may He be exalted! - says:

*"It is not devotion to turn your faces towards the East
or the West. Rather, true devotion is when someone
believes in Allah, and the Last Day, and the Angels, and
the Book, and the Prophets."* (2:177)

Allah - glory be to Him and may He be exalted! - says:

*"The Messenger believes in what has been sent down to
him from his Lord, and so do the believers. Each one
believes in Allah and His angels and His Books and His
Messengers. We do not differentiate between any of His
Messengers."* (2:285)

The Almighty says:

*"Anyone who rejects Allah and His angels and His
Books and His Messengers and the Last Day has gone
very far astray."* (4:136)

In these blessed *ayats*, the Noble Qur'an guides us to the fact
that belief in the angels is a basic tenet of belief. It stands at the
very root of the revelation of Allah and His Messengers because
the revelation of Allah Almighty only reached the Prophet by
means of one of the angels named Jibril, the Trustee of the Revelation. Thus if a person denies the existence of the angels, he also
denies the revelation of the Divine Books and consequently the
message of the Messengers. That is why the Qur'an mentions
belief in the angels before belief in the Divine Books and the Messengers.

3

Anyone who rejects the existence of the angels, according to the way that the Qur'an has clearly described them, is an unbeliever since Allah, the Blessed and Exalted, says:

> *"O you who believe! Believe in Allah and His Messenger, and the Book which He sent down to His Messenger, and the Book which He sent down before. Anyone who rejects Allah and His angels and His Books and His Messengers and the Last Day has gone very far astray."* (4:136)

Thus the Qur'an makes clear the obligation of belief in the angels in these two ways. Firstly by confirming the belief of those who believe in them in the *ayat* of *Surat al-Baqara:* "The Messenger believes...", and secondly by denying belief to those who reject them in the *ayat* in *Surat an-Nisa'* . The Prophet, may Allah bless him and grant him peace, said in a *hadith* transmitted by Muslim, when he was asked about belief:

> "It is that you believe in Allah, His angels, His Books, His Messengers and the Last Day, and that you believe in the Decree, both the good and the bad of it...."

4

The Creation of the Angels

Muslim transmitted in his *Sahih* from 'A'isha, peace be upon her, that the Messenger of Allah, may Allah bless him and grant him peace, said:

"The angels were created from light. The jinn were created from fire. Man was created from what has been described to you."

Ibn Hajar said in the *Fath* and mentioned in *Rabi' al-Abrar* that Sa'id b. al-Musayyab said, "The angels are neither male nor female. They neither eat nor drink. They do not marry nor have children." The angels are free of all animal appetites and are unadulterated by any selfish inclination.

Allah Almighty called the angels "slaves" and honoured them by the fact of their being connected to His name, the All-Merciful. He made it clear that those who think that they are female are not right because they say this with no knowledge. Allah says:

"They have designated the angels female, those who are the slaves of the Merciful. Were they present to witness their creation? Their witnessing will be written down and they will be asked about it." (43:19)

Allah - glory be to Him! - criticised those who described the angels as being female and stripped such people of the attribute of belief, saying:

"Those who do not believe in the Next World name the angels with the names of females. They do not have any

knowledge of it. They only follow supposition, and suppo-
sition is of no avail at all against the Truth." (53:27)

The Wings of the Angels

The Almighty says:

"Praise belongs to Allah, the Bringer-into-being of the
heavens and the earth, the Maker of the angels into mes-
sengers, possessing wings - two, three and four. He adds
to creation in any way He wills. Allah is over all things
powerful." (35:1)

Allah - Glory be to Him! - makes it clear that the angels have
wings. Some of them have two wings, some three, some four, and
some have more than that as has come in a *hadith* saying that the
Messenger of Allah, may Allah bless him and grant him peace,
saw Jibril, peace be upon him, on the Night Journey and he had six
hundred wings, the distance between each wing being the same as
that between the east and the west. This is why Allah - glory be to
Him! - says: *"He adds to creation in any way He wills."* (35:1)
As-Suddi said, "He increases the number of wings and creates
them as He wills." That is the position taken by most of the commentators.

The Magnitude of the Angels

The angels are immense in size, far and away bigger than any
other of the creatures we normally see. That is indicated by the
words of the Almighty:

"O you who believe, guard yourselves and your families
against a Fire whose fuel is men and stones, and over
which are harsh, terrible angels who do not disobey Allah

6

in anything He commands them and do what they are commanded." (66:6)

Imam Muslim reported that Ibn Mas'ud said, "The Messenger of Allah, may Allah bless him and grant him peace, saw Jibril dressed in a green robe and he completely filled all the space between heaven and earth."

The Messenger of Allah, may Allah bless him and grant him peace, reported:

"I was given permission to speak about one of the Bearers of the Throne - his two feet are resting on the lowest earth and the Throne rests on the top of his head. The distance between his ear-lobes and his neck is that of the flight of a bird for seven hundred years. He (i.e. the angel) says, 'Glory be to You wherever You are.'"

The angels vary in size, not being all the same, some of them having two wings, some three and some four, up to Jibril who has six hundred wings.

The Beauty of the Angels

Allah - Glory be to Him! - created the angels with a noble beautiful form, as He - glory be to Him! - says in respect of Jibril, the Trustee of Revelation:

"Taught him by one terrible in power, very strong (dhu marra) He stood poised" (53:6)

Ibn 'Abbas said that *"dhu marra"* in this *ayat* means "having a beautiful appearance" It is commonly established knowledge that the angels are beautiful in form, just as it is also commonly established that the satans are ugly. That is why people say that a beautiful human being looks like an angel. Look at what the women said about Yusuf when they saw him:

7

"When they saw him, they were amazed by him and cut their hands. They said, 'Allah preserve! This is no man. This is but a noble angel standing here!'" (12:31)

The Number of the Angels

The Almighty says:

"The heavens nearly split above them when the angels glorify the praise of their Lord and ask forgiveness for those on the earth." (42:5)

And He says:

"None knows the hosts of your Lord except Him." (74:31)

There are untold myriads of angels who have been created. No one knows their number except for Him who created them. If you want to have an idea of how great their number is, simply listen to this *hadith*. The Prophet, may Allah bless him and grant him peace, said:

"The heaven groans and it has a right to groan." He, may Allah bless him and grant him peace, said, "On that day Jahannam will be drawn up by 70,000 thongs, and holding each thong there will be 70,000 angels."

According to that, the angels who bring *Jahannam* on the Day of Rising will alone number 4,900,000,000.

If you reflect on the texts related about the angels who take care of each member of mankind, you will understand the hugeness of their number. There is the angel in charge of each sperm drop, two angels to record, guardian angels and also the two angels accompanying each human being to guide and direct him.

The Worship and Glorification of the Angels

The Almighty says:

"Those who bear the Throne, and all those around it, glorify the praise of their Lord and believe in Him and ask forgiveness for those who believe: "Our Lord, You encompass everything in mercy and knowledge! Forgive those who turn to You and who follow Your way and safeguard them from the punishment of the Blazing Fire." (40:7)

He - glory be to Him! - says:

"You will see the angels circling round the Throne, glorifying the praise of their Lord." (39:75)

The Mighty and Majestic says that the angels say:

"We are those drawn up in ranks. We are those who glorify." (37:165-166)

In the *hadith* transmitted by at-Tabarani, Jabir, may Allah be pleased with him said:

"The Messenger of Allah, may Allah bless him and grant him peace, said, 'There is no space in the seven heavens a foot's length or a hand-span or a palm's width which does not have an angel standing, bowing or prostrating on it.'"

The Frequented House

It is confirmed in the two *Sahih* collections that the Messenger of Allah, may Allah bless him and grant him peace, said in the *hadith* of the Night Journey after his visit to the seventh heaven:

9

"Then I was taken up to the Frequented House and every day 70,000 angels visit it, never returning to it again, another [group] coming after them."

In other words they worship and do *tawaf* there just as the people of the earth do *tawaf* of their *Ka'ba*.

Al-'Awfi said that Ibn 'Abbas said, "It is a house opposite the Throne. The angels visit it and pray in it, 70,000 angels every day, and then never return to it again." That is similar to what 'Ikrima, Mujahid and several of the *Salaf* said.

Muhammad ibn al-Munkadir said, "When the Fire was created, the hearts of the angels flew away out of fear. When Adam was created, they returned to their places."

It is reported that when Iblis did what he did, Jibril and Mika'il began to weep. Then Allah Almighty revealed to them, "What is this weeping?" They said, "O Lord, even we are not safe from Your devising." The Almighty said, "That then is how you are."

O my God!

There is no lord in existence who
   is worshipped except for You!

No indeed! And no protector
   to seek safety with apart from You!

O You to whom all faces are humbled
   and whose oneness all beings declare,

You are the One Unique God whom
   all hearts affirm and all bear witness to.

The Story of Adam and the Angels

The Almighty says:

"When your Lord said to the angels, 'I am placing a khalif on the earth.' They said, 'Why place on it one who will corrupt it and shed blood, when we glorify Your praise and call You holy?' He said, 'I know what You do not know.' He taught Adam all the names. Then He displayed them to the angels and said, 'Tell me the names of these if you are telling the truth.' They said, 'Glory be to You! We have no knowledge except what You have taught us. You are the Knowing, the Wise.' He said, 'Adam, tell them their names.' When he had told them their names He said, 'Did I not tell you that I know the Unseen of the heavens and the earth, and I know all that you make known and all you conceal?' When We said to the angels, 'Prostrate yourselves to Adam!' They prostrated, all except Iblis. He disdained to and grew arrogant and was one of the rejectors." (2:30-34)

The angels existed before Adam and his descendants for a long period which is known only to Allah - glory be to Him. When Allah wished to make Adam and his descendants His representatives on earth, He informed the angels about it. It may be that the wisdom in telling them lay in the fact that after Adam was created, the angels would then be linked to this creature and his descendants. Then they were commanded to show him honour and esteem by prostrating to him as a test of their obedience.

Allah had decreed that some of the angels would be guardians and scribes and others angels of revelation, rain and plant-growth, punishment and death. All of them are linked to the life of human beings and what is decreed for them and their final destiny. The

11

answer which the angels gave to this divine news about the creation of Adam was not in any way an objection. The wisdom of this new creation was hidden from them and they wanted to learn what it was. They described man as corrupting the earth and shedding blood before he existed because they grasped that, since this creature would be made of clay and would live on the earth, he must have a nature which would entail both good and evil. Therefore there would inevitably be dispute and strife between his descendants and thus corruption and bloodshed.

When the angels perceived the special properties possessed by this new creature and recognised his predisposition for gnosis and the great quantity of knowledge with which Allah had provided him, they prostrated with a prostration of greeting and honour in obedience to the command of Allah Almighty:

"When We said to the angels, 'Prostrate yourselves to Adam!' They prostrated, all except Iblis. He disdained to and grew arrogant and was one of the rejectors."

Thus Shaytan is the accursed one who made an analogy using his defective intellect and said, "I am better than him. You created me from fire and You created him from clay." (38:76) He did not obey the divine command as the angels had done and so he deserved to fall into error and to be driven away from mercy. Iblis was not one of the angels. He was one of the jinn as the Qur'an makes clear:

"When We said to the angels, 'Prostrate yourselves to Adam,' They prostrated except for Iblis. He was one of the jinn and wantonly deviated from his Lord's command." (18:50)

Adam's Greeting to the Angels

When Allah created Adam, He said to him, "Go and greet that group," referring to a group of angels who were sitting there. "Listen to the greeting they give you in return. It is your greeting and the greeting of your descendants." So he went and said, "Peace be upon you," and they said, "Peace be upon you and the mercy of Allah." The Prophet, may Allah bless him and grant him peace, said, "They added, 'and the mercy of Allah.'" Muslim relates the *hadith*.

The Different Types of Angels

Jibril, Mika'il and Israfil

The angels are the greatest of all the hosts of Allah - glory be to Him and may He be exalted! They include the angel who is entrusted with the revelation from Allah Almighty to His Messengers, blessings and peace be upon them. He is the Faithful Spirit, Jibril, peace be upon him. The Almighty says:

> "The Faithful Spirit brought it down upon your heart for you to be one of the Warners in a clear Arabic tongue."
> (26:193-195)

They include the angel entrusted with the rain and dispensing it wherever Allah, the Almighty and Majestic, commands him to. He is Mika'il, peace be upon him. He possesses a high position, a lofty station and great honour with his Lord, the Almighty and Majestic. He has helpers who do everything he orders them to by the command of his Lord. They make the winds and clouds move as Allah, the Almighty and Majestic, wishes. It says in the *hadith* of Ibn 'Abbas in at-Tabarani that the Prophet, may Allah bless him and grant him peace, said to Jibril:

> "What is Mika'il in charge of?" He replied, "The plants and the rain."

Imam Ahmad transmitted in his *Musnad* from Anas b. Malik, may Allah be pleased with him, that the Prophet, may Allah bless him and grant him peace, said to Jibril, peace be upon him:

> "Why do I never see Mika'il laugh?" He replied, "Mika'il has not laughed since the Fire was created."

14

They include the angel entrusted with the Trumpet. He is Israfil, peace be upon him. He will blow three blasts on it at the command of His Lord, the Almighty and Majestic. The first is the Blast of Terror, the second the Blast of Swooning, and the third the Blast of the Rising for the Lord of heaven and earth. Imam Ahmad and at-Tirmidhi transmitted that Abu Sa'id al-Khudri said that the Messenger of Allah, may Allah bless him and grant him peace, said:

> "How can I enjoy myself when the one with the Trumpet has raised the Trumpet to his mouth, knitted his brow and is waiting to blow." They said, "What should we say, Messenger of Allah?" He said, "Say: Allah is enough for us and the best Guardian. We have put our trust in Allah."

These noble three – Jibril, Mika'il and Israfil - are the leaders of the angels. The Prophet, may Allah bless him and grant him peace, used to say in his supplication:

> "O Allah, Lord of Jibril, Mika'il and Israfil, Bringer of the heavens and the earth into being, Knower of the unseen and visible, it is You who judges between Your slaves concerning the things about which they disagree. Guide us to the truth in respect of the things about which there is disagreement by Your permission. You guide whomever You will to a straight path."

Ibn al-Qayyim, may Allah have mercy on him, said, "The Messenger of Allah, may Allah bless him and grant him peace, pleaded with Allah - Glory be to Him! - by His overall lordship and His particular lordship over these three angels who are the guardians of all life. Jibril is entrusted with the revelation by which hearts and souls are brought to life; Mika'il is entrusted with the rain by which land, plants and animals are brought to life; and Israfil is entrusted with blowing the Trumpet by which all creatures will be brought to life after their death. Therefore Allah's Messenger asked Allah by His lordship over these angels to guide him to the truth in respect of those things about which there is disagreement by His permission since in that lies all the benefits of life.

The Angel of Death

Another of the angels is entrusted with the taking of the souls. He is the Angel of Death and his helpers. Some reports call him 'Azra'il. Allah Almighty says:

> *"Say: 'The Angel of Death will take you back, who has been given charge of you. Then you will be returned unto your Lord.'"* (32:11)

The Almighty says about the hypocrites:

> *"How will it be when the angels take them, beating their faces and their backs."* (47:27)

And He says about the believer:

> *"Those the angels take in a good and wholesome state. They say, 'Peace be upon you! Enter the Garden on account of the things you were doing.'"* (16:32)

It has come in sound *hadiths* that the helpers of this angel come to the dying person according to his actions. If he is a good-doer, then they have the best appearance and most beautiful form and bring the greatest good news. If he is evil, then they take on the ugliest appearance and most atrocious aspect and bear the harshest threat. Then they draw out the soul until it reaches the dying person's throat where the Angel of Death takes it. They do not leave it in his hands, but wrap it in shrouds and the appropriate perfume. As the Almighty says:

> *"Why, but when the soul leaps to the throat of the dying man and that hour you are watching. And We are nearer*

16

to him than you, but you do not see Us. Why, if you are not at Our disposal, do you not bring back his soul, if you speak the truth? Then, if he be one of those brought nigh the Throne, there shall be repose and ease, and a Garden of Delight. And if he be a Companion of the Right, 'Peace be upon you, Companion of the Right!' And if he be of them that cried lies and went astray, there shall be a hospitality of boiling water and the roasting of the Blaze. Surely this is the truth of certainty. Then magnify the Name of your Lord, the All-mighty." (56:83-96)

The Guardian Angels

Another type of angel are those entrusted with guarding each person both at home and while travelling, in his sleep and when awake, and in all his states. They are those who take over from one another. Allah Almighty says:

"It makes no difference whether you keep secret what you say or voice it out loud, whether you hide in the night or go out in the day. Each has a succession of angels in front and behind, keeping him safe by Allah's command." (13:10-11)

The Almighty says:

"He is the Absolute Master over His slaves. He sends angels to watch over you." (6:61)

Ibn 'Abbas said about the first *ayat, "Each has a succession of angels in front and behind, keeping him safe by Allah's command"* that *'the succession of angels'* from Allah refer to the angels who protect him in front and behind. When Allah's decree comes, they leave him. Mujahid said, "There is no one who does not have an angel who is entrusted with protecting him both when asleep and when awake, from jinn and men and reptiles. None of them comes

17

to him without finding an angel blocking its way except for something which Allah has given permission to reach him."

The Recording Angels

They also include the angels entrusted with preserving the record of each person's good and evil actions. These are the noble scribes and are included in the words of the Almighty:

"He sends angels to watch over you."

The Almighty also says:

"Or do they reckon that We do not hear their secrets and private conversation? Indeed, Our messengers are with them writing it down." (43:80)

And He says:

"When the two angels meet together, sitting one on the right, and one on the left, not a word he utters, but by him is an observer ready at hand." (50:17)

The one on his right is the one who writes down good actions, and the one on his left is the one who writes down evil actions. The Almighty further says:

"Yet there are over you noble watchers, writers who know whatever you do." (82:11)

Ibn Abi Hatim transmits with his *isnad* from Mujahid that the Messenger of Allah, may Allah bless him and grant him peace, said:

"Honour the noble scribes who only leave you at two times: in *janaba* and when you relieve yourselves. When

18

one of you has a *ghusl*, he should screen himself with a wall or his camel, or his brother should screen him."

Sufyan was asked, "How do the angels know that a person intends a good or evil action?" He replied, "When someone intends a good action, they smell the scent of musk coming from him, and when he intends an evil action, they smell a putrid smell coming from him. Al-Bukhari transmitted with his *isnad* from Abu Hurayra, may Allah be pleased with him, that the Messenger of Allah, may Allah bless him and grant him peace, said:

"Allah, the Mighty and Majestic, has said, 'When My slave wants to do an evil action, you should not write it down until he does it. If he does it, then write down the equivalent of it. If he does not do it for My sake, then write it down as a good action for him. If he wants to do a good action and does not do it, then write it down as a good action. If he does do it, then write down ten to seven hundred of its like.'"

Ibn Hajar said in *al-Fath,* "This *hadith* indicates that the angel is aware of what is in the heart of the human being, either by Allah acquainting him with it or by creating for him knowledge by which he perceives it." Al-Hasan al-Basri said about the *ayat*:

"When the two angels meet together, sitting one on the right, and one on the left, not a word he utters, but by him is an observer ready at hand." (50:17)

"O son of Adam! A scroll has been unfurled for you and two noble angels have been entrusted with you, one on your right and the other on your left. The one on your right records your good actions. The one on your left records your evil actions. So do what you wish, whether it is a little or a lot. Then, when you die, your scroll will be rolled up and placed by your neck with you in your grave until you emerge on the Day of Rising. Then Allah Almighty will say:*'We have fastened the destiny of every man

19

about his neck and on the Day of Rising We will extract a book for
him which he will find spread open in front of him. "Read your
book! Today your own self is reckoner enough against you!"
(17:13-14) Then he said, "It is just, by Allah. In you is the one
who makes you your own reckoner."

Al-Bukhari transmitted with his *isnad* from Abu Hurayra, may
Allah be pleased with him, that the Messenger of Allah, may Allah
bless him and grant him peace, said:

> "The angels of the night and the angels of the day take
> turns in attending you and they meet at the *'Asr* prayer and
> the *Fajr* prayer. Then those who spent the night with you
> ascend and He questions them, although He knows better
> than them. He says, 'How did you leave My slaves?' They
> say, 'We left them while they were praying and we came
> to them while they were praying.'"

He also transmitted from Abu Musa, may Allah be pleased with
him, who said:

> "The Messenger of Allah, may Allah bless him and
> grant him peace, stood up in our midst and made four
> statements. He said, 'Allah does not sleep and it is not
> proper for Him to sleep; He lessens and increases what is
> allotted to you; the actions of the night are presented to
> Him before the actions of the day; and the actions of the
> day are presented to Him before the actions of the night."

Munkar and Nakir

Among the angels are also those who are in charge of the trial
of the grave. They are called Munkar and Nakir. Al-Bukhari, may
Allah have mercy on him, transmitted from Anas, may Allah be
pleased with him, that the Prophet, may Allah bless him and grant
him peace, said:

"When someone is placed in his grave, and his companions turn and go, and he can still hear the tread of their sandals, two angels come to him and make him sit up and say to him, 'What do you say about this man, Muhammad, may Allah bless him and grant him peace?' He will say, 'I testify that he is the slave of Allah and His Messenger.' It will be said, 'Look at your place in the Fire. Allah has given you, in exchange for it, a place in the Garden.'" The Prophet said, "He will see both places."

"The unbeliever or the hypocrite will say, 'I do not know. I used to say what everyone else said.' He will be told, 'You neither understood nor followed the guidance.' Then he will be hit between the ears with an iron hammer and will cry out with a cry which is heard by everything near him except men and *jinn*."

Muslim reported something similar to it from Qatada and he added in it that Qatada said, "He mentioned to us that the believer's grave will be expanded to about seventy cubits for him, and it will be filled with greenery until the day they are brought back to life."

Muslim transmitted from 'Abdullah b. 'Abbas that the Messenger of Allah, may Allah bless him and grant him peace, used to teach them this supplication in the same way that he used to teach them a *sura* of Qur'an. He would say:

"O Allah, I seek refuge with You from the punishment of Jahannam and I seek refuge with You from the punishment of the grave. I seek refuge with You from the trial of the *Masih ad-Dajjal* and I seek refuge with You from the trials of life and death."

The Custodians of the Garden and the Fire

There are other angels who are the custodians of the Garden. Their overseer is called Ridwan, peace be upon him. Allah Almighty says:

*"And those who were fearful of their Lord will be driven
to the Garden in companies and then, when they arrive
there finding its gates open, its custodians will say to
them, 'Peace be upon you! You have done well so enter it
timelessly forever.'"* (39:71)

Ibn Kathir said, "The custodian of the Garden is an angel called
Ridwan. This is explicitly stated in some *hadiths*."

There are also angels whose task is to give good news to the
believers both at the time of their death and on the Day of Rising,
as the Almighty says:

*"Those who say, 'Our Lord is Allah,' and then go
straight, the angels descend on them, 'Feel no fear and do
not be sad but rejoice in the Garden which you were
promised. We are your protectors in the life of this world
and in the Next World. You will have there all your selves
could wish for. You will have there all that you demand.
Hospitality from One who is forgiving, most merciful.'"*
(41:30-32)

Ibn Abi Hatim said in his *isnad* from Ja'far ibn Sulayman who
said that he heard Thabit recite *Surat Fussilat* until he reached,
*"Those who say, 'Our Lord is Allah,' and then go straight, the
angels descend on them."* Then he stopped and said, "It has
reached us that when Allah Almighty raises the believing slave
from his grave, he will be met by the two angels who were with
him in this world. They will say to him, *'Feel no fear and do not
be sad but rejoice in the Garden which you were promised."* He
said, "Allah will give him security from his fear and delight his
eye. None of the terrible things which people fear on the Day of
Rising will be anything other than a delight for a believer due to
the fact that Allah Almighty guided him, and on account of what
he used to do for Him in this world."

They also include the custodians of *Jahannam*. We seek refuge
with Allah from them! Its overseer is Malik, peace be upon him
and them.

The Almighty says about the people of the Fire:

"They will call out, 'O Malik, let your Lord finish us off!' He will say, 'You will remain.'" (43:77)

The Almighty says:

"Those who are in the Fire will say to the custodians of Jahannam, 'Call on your Lord to make lighter for us one day of the punishment. They will say, 'Did your Messengers not bring you the Clear Signs?' They will say, 'Yes.' They will say, 'Then you call!' But the calling of those who reject only goes astray." (40:49-50)

The Almighty says:

"O you who believe, safeguard yourselves and your families against a Fire whose fuel is men and stones, and over which are harsh, terrible angels who do not disobey Allah in anything He commands them and do what they are commanded." (66:6)

The Almighty says:

"What will teach you what is Saqar? It spares not, nor does it cease to scorch the flesh. Over it are nineteen. We have not appointed any but angels to be masters of the Fire, and We have appointed their number only as a trial for the unbelievers." (74:27-31)

It is said that the leaders of the custodians of *Jahannam* are nineteen angels and that their overseer is Malik, peace be upon him.

We find in the *Sahih* of Muslim, "On the Day of Rising, *Jahannam* will be drawn up by 70,000 thongs, and on each thong there will be 70,000 angels."

23

Angels entrusted with the sperm in the womb

There are also the angels entrusted with dealing with the sperm in the womb. From 'Abdullah b. Mas'ud, may Allah be pleased with him, who said, "The Messenger of Allah, may Allah bless him and grant him peace, whose truthfulness is confirmed, said:

'The way that each of you is created is that you are gathered in your mother's womb for forty days as a sperm-drop and then for a similar length of time as a blood-clot and then for a similar length of time as a lump of flesh. Then an angel is sent and he breathes the spirit into you and is charged with four commands: to write down your provision, your life-span, your actions, and whether you will be wretched or happy.'"

Al-Bukhari and Muslim both reported this, and the two of them also transmitted from Anas b. Malik, may Allah be pleased with him, that he said that the Messenger of Allah, may Allah bless him and grant him peace, said:

"Allah has put an angel in charge of the womb. He says, 'O Lord, a drop? O Lord, a clot? O Lord, a morsel?' When Allah desires to complete the creation of the foetus, he says, 'O Lord, male or female? Wretched or happy? How much provision? How long a lifespan?' and he writes that for him in his mother's womb."

It is also related that these scribes write this between the eyes of the foetus. In the *isnad* of al-Bazzar from Ibn 'Umar, may Allah be pleased with both him and his father, is that the Prophet, may Allah bless him and grant him peace, said:

"When Allah creates a living soul, the angel of the wombs says, 'O Lord, male or female?'" He said, "Allah decides it for him. Then he says, 'O Lord, wretched or happy?' And Allah decides it for him. Then he writes

between his eyes all he will encounter until his end over-
takes him."

The Bearers of the Throne

Also included are the Bearers of the Throne. Allah Almighty
says:

*"Upon that day eight shall bear above them the Throne
of your Lord."* (69:17)

Ibn 'Abbas said that it means eight rows of angels.
From Jabir ibn 'Abdullah, may Allah be pleased with both him
and his father, is that the Messenger of Allah, may Allah bless him
and grant him peace, said:

"I was given permission to report about one of the
angels of Allah Almighty among the Throne-bearers that
between his ear-lobe and his neck is the distance of seven
hundred years."

The Karubiyyun

They include another category called the *Karubiyyun*. They are
the chiefs of the angels who are brought near and are the closest
angels to the Throne-bearers.
The word *"karubiyyun"* comes from the root of *"karb"* which
means sorrow, and they are called this on account of the intensity
of their fear of Allah Almighty and their awe of Him. It is also said
that the word is derived from the expression *"kurb"* meaning near-
ness or strength in which case the name is due to their strength and
steadfastness in worship.

The Angel of the Mountains

Another one is the angel entrusted with the mountains. He is mentioned in the *hadith* when the Prophet, may Allah bless him and grant him peace, went out at night to visit the Banu 'Abd and returned from them. That *hadith* contains the statement of Jibril to him:

"Allah has heard what your people said to you and the reply they gave you. He has sent the Angel of the mountains with me so that you can command him as you wish. If you wish, he will crush your people by causing the mountains to fall on top of them, or if you wish, he will make the earth swallow them up." The Prophet, may Allah bless him and grant him peace, said, "Give them more time. Hopefully Allah will bring forth from their loins people who will worship Allah without associating anyone else with Him."

The Angels of the Ranks

They include the angels of the ranks who do not slacken in worship, those who stand and do not bow, those who bow, and those who prostrate and do not come up from their prostration. And there are others who are different from any of these:

"None knows the hosts of your Lord except Him. It is nothing but a reminder to all human beings." (74:31)

Imam Ahmad reports in his *Musnad,* as does at-Tirmidhi, from Abu Dharr, may Allah be pleased with him, that the Messenger of Allah, may Allah bless him and grant him peace, said:

"I see what you do not see and I hear what you do not hear. The heaven groans and it has a right to groan. There is no place in it the size of four fingers which does not

26

have an angel prostrating in it. If you knew what I knew, you would laugh little and weep much and not enjoy women in your beds and you would go out to the hill crying out to Allah, the Mighty and Majestic."

The meaning of "the heaven groans" is that it makes the sound of the creaking of a saddle which is placed on the camel's back, i.e. due to the great number of the angels in it, which weighs it down so that it groans.

The Angels of *dhikr*

Yet another type are the travelling angels who seek gatherings of *dhikr*. It is related that Abu Hurayra, may Allah be pleased with him, said that the Messenger of Allah, may Allah bless him and grant him peace, said:

"Allah Almighty has angels who roam about seeking the people of *dhikr*. When they find a group doing *dhikr* of Allah, they call to one another, 'Come to that which you have been seeking!' And they beat their wings and fly up to the nearest heaven. Then their Lord questions them - and He knows better - 'What do My slaves say?' They say, 'They glorify and proclaim You great, praise you and magnify You.' Then He says, 'Have they seen Me?' Then they say, 'No, by Allah, they have not seen You.' Then He says, 'And how would it be if they did see Me?' They say, 'If they did see You, they would be even stronger in worshipping You, stronger in glorifying You, and stronger in magnifying You.' He says, 'And what do they ask of Me?' They say, 'They ask You for the Garden.' He says, 'And have they seen it?' They say, 'No, by Allah, they have not seen it.' He says, 'Then how would it be if they had seen it?' They say, 'If they had seen it, they would be all the stronger in their striving for it, stronger in their seeking it, and stronger in their desire for it.' He says, 'Then from

27

what do they seek deliverance?' They say, 'From the Fire.'
He says, 'Then how would it be if they saw it?' They say,
'If they saw it, they would be the stronger in their flight
from it and stronger in their fear of it.' He says, 'I call you
to witness that I have forgiven them.' One of the angels
says, 'Among them is so-and-so, and he is not one of
them. He has only come for something which he needs.'
He said, 'They are companions of whom it can be said that
no one who is their companion will be wretched.'"

Al-Bukhari and Muslim

Ibn Hajar said in the *Fath al-Bari*, "This *hadith* shows the
excellence of gatherings of *dhikr* and those who do *dhikr*, and the
excellence of people gathering together for that reason, as well as
the fact that anyone who sits with them is included along with
them in all that Allah Almighty bestows on them to honour them,
even if he does not participate with them in the *dhikr* itself. It also
shows the love and concern of the angels for the tribe of Adam. It
also contains the fact that the questioner comes to the One who
asks even though He has better knowledge of the one He asks
about than the one who is asked. This is in order to show His concern for those He asks about, to praise their ability and to proclaim
the nobility of their station.

"It is said that another of the features of Allah's asking the
angels about the people of *dhikr* is to call attention to what they
said when they said, '*Why place on it one who will corrupt it and
shed blood when we glorify Your praise and call You holy?*' (2:30)
So it is as if He were saying to them, 'Look at the glorification and
proclamation of Your holiness that comes from them in spite of the
appetites and the whisperings of Shaytan which overpower them.
See how they deal with that and yet resemble you in respect of
glorification and holy praise.'

"It is said that also taken from this *hadith* is that the *dhikr* of
the tribe of Adam is more sublime and nobler than that of the
angels since those descended from Adam manage to do *dhikr* in
spite of the many preoccupations they have and the transactions
they are involved in, while none of that is the case where the

angels are concerned."

Angels of Visions

There are also angels connected with visions. Al-Bukhari transmitted that 'A'isha, may Allah be pleased with her, said that the Prophet, may Allah bless him and grant him peace, said:

"I saw you twice in a dream before I married you. I saw an angel carrying you wrapped in a piece of silk and I said, 'Unwrap it!' and it was unwrapped and there you were. I said, 'If this is from Allah, it will come about.'"

Ibn Hajar said, "Al-Qurtubi transmitted in *al-Mufham* from one of the people of knowledge that Allah Almighty has an angel who presents the things seen in the sleeper's domain of perception and gives them a sensory form, so that sometimes they are likenesses which correspond to already existing forms, and sometimes they are examples of intelligible meanings. In both cases there is either good news or warning."

Al-Hakim at-Tirmidhi said, "Allah has entrusted an angel with the business of visions. He learns the states of the tribe of Adam from the Preserved Tablet, and then he copies from it and coins a likeness of each according to a particular archetype. When a person sleeps, he gives form to those things for him with wisdom so that it will be good news or warning or rebuke for him.

The Adamic creature is overpowered by Shaytan due to the intense enmity which exists between him and Shaytan, and so he tricks him in every possible way and wants to corrupt his affair in every possible way. Therefore he muddles up his dreams, either by putting error into them or by making him forget them."

Ibn Hajar said, "All dreams fall into two categories. The first are true dreams, which are the dreams of the Prophets and those of the righteous who follow them. They occur to others in rare cases. This is the type of dream when what happens in it corresponds to what happens in the waking state. The second consists of muddled

29

dreams which are dreams which do not warn about anything. There are different types of these.

One is the playing-about of Shaytan so that the dream is troubling. For instance someone might see his head cut off and himself chasing it or dream that he falls into a state of terror and has no one to rescue him from it and other such-like things. Another is when someone sees one of the angels commanding him to do something *haram*, for instance. Dreams like this present logical impossibilities.

A third is when someone sees the same sort of things his self says to him when he is awake or that he desires something and sees it when he is asleep, like when he dreams of something which normally occurs in the waking state or of something that dominates his nature. This kind of dream occurs mostly about the future, sometimes about the present and only rarely about the past."

Different Forms in which Angels Appear

The angels can take a shape other than their true form and appear in whatever excellent form they wish. They appear to a selected elite of the slaves of Allah, frequently in the shape of extraordinary men with handsome forms and shining faces and excellent clothes. However, the bodies they take on when adopting human form do not remove them from the basic nature they were given by Allah when He created them. Thus when, for instance, they take on human form, human nature does not have any power over them. They do not, for example, eat or drink.

The angels appeared to the Close Friend of the Merciful, Ibrahim, peace be upon him, in this Adamic form which led him, due to the impulse of generosity rooted in his basic nature, to hasten to offer them hospitality, thinking that they were ordinary guests. They came to him to visit him. Allah Almighty says:

> "Has there come to you the story of the honoured guests of Ibrahim? When they entered upon him, saying, 'Peace!' he said 'Peace! You are a people unknown to me.' Then he turned to his household and brought a fattened calf and he laid it before them, saying, 'Will you not eat?' Then he conceived a fear of them. They said, 'Do not be afraid!' And they gave him the good tidings of a cunning boy. Then his wife came forward, clamouring, and she smote her face and said, 'An old woman, barren!' They said, 'So says thy Lord. He is the All-Wise, the All-Knowing.' He said, 'And what is your business, envoys?' They said, 'We have been sent to a people of sinners, to loose upon them stones of clay marked with your Lord for the prodigal.'" (51:24-34)

31

When they visited Lut, the angels took the shape of handsome, beardless youths. He felt terrible constriction on their account and unable to offer them hospitality. That was because he was afraid that his people would violate them. So the Almighty says:

"When Our messengers came to Lut, he was distressed on their account, feeling unequipped to help them, and said, 'This is a dreadful day.' His people came running excitedly to him. They were long used to committing acts of wrong. He said, 'O my people! Here are my daughters. They are purer for you. So be fearful of Allah. Do not disgrace me in respect of my guests. Is there not one rightly-guided man among you?' They said, 'You know we have no claim to your daughters. You know very well what we want.' He said, 'If only I had the strength to combat you or could take refuge in some powerful support!' They said, 'Lut, we are messengers of your Lord. They will not get to you. Set out with your family in a watch of the night and let not any of you look back - excepting your wife. What smites them will smite her. Their promised appointment is the morning. Is the morning not near-at-hand?' When Our command came, We turned the place upside down and rained down upon it stones of baked clay, piled on top of one another, each one marked by your Lord, and they are never far from the wrongdoers." (11:77-83)

The Story of Maryam

The noble Qur'an reports to us:

"When the angels said, 'Maryam! Your Lord gives you good news of a word from Him. His name is the Messiah, 'Isa, son of Maryam, of high standing in this world and the Next World, one of those brought near. He will speak to people in the cradle and when full-grown, and will be one of the righteous." (3:45-46)

Jibril, peace be upon him, took the form of a well-built fully mature man because she would have been unable to look at him in his true form. The Almighty says:

"Recall in the Book Maryam, when she withdrew from her people to a place towards the east, and screened herself away from them. Then We sent Our spirit to her and it took on for her the form of a handsome well-built man." (19:16-17)

When she saw in front of her a young man of handsome form and beautiful countenance who had pierced the veil to reach her, she thought that he meant to do her harm. She was chaste and pure as Allah had brought her up. Therefore she sought refuge with Allah to protect her from him:

"She said, 'I seek refuge from you with the All-Merciful if you are Godfearing.' He said, 'I am but your Lord's messenger so that He can give you a pure boy.' She said, 'How can I have a boy when no man has touched me and I am not a loose woman?' He said, 'Just like that! Your Lord says, 'That is easy for Me. So that We can make him a sign for mankind and a mercy from Us. It is a matter already decreed.'" (19:18-21)

Sometimes the angels take the form of ordinary people and contact certain people to inform them of what will make things easier for them and to expand their breasts to good deeds, praiseworthy actions and noble character. Muslim reported in his *Sahih* from Abu Hurayra, may Allah be pleased with him, that the Prophet, may Allah bless him and grant him peace, said:

"A man visited a brother of his in another town and Allah delegated an angel to guard him on his way. When he came to him, the angel said, 'Where are you going?' He said, 'I am going to visit a brother of mine in that town.' He said, 'Do you have any property with him that you want to check on?' He said, 'No, it is only that I love him for the sake of Allah.' He said, 'I am the messenger of Allah to you to tell you that Allah loves you as you love this man for His sake.'"

Angels Being Sent to Test Mankind

Al-Bukhari and Muslim report that Abu Hurayra heard the Messenger of Allah, may Allah bless him and grant him peace say:

"Three of the Tribe of Isra'il were respectively leprous, bald and blind. Allah wanted to put them to the test and so he sent an angel to them. He came to the leper and said, 'What is the thing you would like best?' He said, 'A good complexion and clear skin and for the thing that I have which makes people find me unclean to be taken from me.' He wiped him and his impurity left him and he gave him a good complexion. He said, 'What form of wealth do you like best?' He said, 'Camels,' and he gave him a pregnant she-camel, saying, 'May Allah bless you in it.'

"Then he came to the bald man and said, 'What is the thing you would like best?' He said, 'A good head of hair and to have what people consider distasteful about me removed from me.' So he touched him and removed what he had and gave him a thick head of hair. He said, 'What form of wealth do you like best?' He said, 'Cattle.' So he gave him a pregnant cow and said, 'May Allah bless you in it.'

"Then he went to the blind man and said, 'What is the thing you would like best?' He said, 'For Allah to return my sight to me so that I can see people.' He touched him and Allah returned his sight to him. He said, 'What form of wealth do you like best?' He said, 'Sheep.' So he gave him a pregnant sheep.

"These animals all gave birth and produced offspring. In time one had a valley full of camels, the other a valley full of cattle and the third a valley full of sheep.

"Then he (the angel) went to the leper, taking on the form that he himself had previously had, and said, 'I am a poor man who has lost his means on his journey. Today I can seek help from none but Allah and then you. I ask you, by the One who gave you a good complexion and good skin and wealth, for a camel so that I can complete my journey.' He said, 'I have many obligations.' He said, 'I seem to recognise you. Were you not a leper, that people found unclean, and poor and then Allah was generous to you?' He said, 'I inherited this property, elder son from elder son.' He said, 'If you are a liar in your claim, may Allah return you to your original state'

"He then went to the bald man, taking on the form that he himself had previously had, and said to him the same as he had said to the other and he replied to him in the same way. He said, 'If you are a liar, may Allah return you to your original state!'

"Finally he went to the blind man and said, 'I am a poor man who has lost his means on his journey. Today I can seek help from no one but Allah and then you. I ask you by the One who returned your sight to you for a sheep so I can complete my journey.' He said, 'I was blind and Allah restored my sight to me, so take what you want and leave what you want. By Allah, I will not be hard on you about anything which you take for Allah, the Mighty and Exalted (i.e. I will not be hard on you by refusing anything you ask of me or take).' He said, 'Keep your wealth. You have been tested and Allah is pleased with you and angry with your companions.'"

The Angel of Death coming to Musa in Human Form

Al-Bukhari transmits with his *isnad* from Abu Hurayra, may Allah be pleased with him, who said, "The angel of death was sent to Musa, peace be upon him. When he came, Musa gave him a

35

black eye so he returned to his Lord and said, 'You sent me to a slave who does not want to die.' Allah restored his eye and said, 'Go back and tell him to put his hand on the back of an ox and he will live a year for every hair that his hand covers.' Musa said, 'O Lord, then what?' He said, 'Then death.' He said, 'Then let it be now.'"

Ibn Hajar said in *al-Fath*, "His words, 'gave him a black eye' means that he hit him in the eye. In another variant in Muslim, it has, 'The angel of death came to Musa and said, 'Answer your Lord!' Musa hit the Angel of Death in the eye and put it out.' In a variant of Abu Hurayra in Ahmad ibn Hanbal and at-Tabarani, we find: 'The angel of death used to come to people in a visible form. He went to Musa and he put out his eye.'"

Ibn Khuzayma said, "Some of the heretics refuse to acknowledge this and say that if Musa recognised him, he did not take him seriously. If he did not recognise him, then how would he not have retaliation from him for putting out his eye? The answer is that Allah did not send the Angel of Death to Musa desiring to take his soul at that moment, He sent him to him to test him. Musa punched the Angel of Death because he thought that he was a human who had entered his house without his permission and did not know that he was the Angel of Death. The *Shari'a* allows for the putting out of the eye of anyone who looks into a Muslim's house without permission. The angels came to Ibrahim and to Lut in human form and they also did not recognise them at first. If Ibrahim had recognised them, he would not have offered them food. If Lut had recognised them he would not have feared for them from his people."

One of the people of knowledge said, "He hit him because he came to take his soul before giving him a choice since it is established that no Prophet is taken without being given a choice. This is why, when he gave him a choice the second time, he submitted."

Ibn Hajar said, "And Ibn Qutayba said, 'Musa put out an eye which was imaginary and symbolic and not a real eye. The meaning of Allah's restoring his eye, is returning him to his true form. It is said that it was only his outward form and that Allah restored his human eye to the Angel of Death so that he could return to Musa in a perfect form. That is the stronger interpretation and is the most reliable one.'"

Ibn Hajar then said, "There are lessons in the *hadith*: for instance, the angel can take on human form. There are also a number of other *hadiths* that show this."

The Story of Harut and Marut

There are some Jewish sources which contain the story of Harut and Marut. As-Suyuti reports in *ad-Durr al-Manthur* commentating on the words of Allah Almighty in *Surat al-Baqara*, *"what had been sent down to the two angels in Babylon, Harut and Marut...."* (2:102): "There are many transmissions and extraordinary stories related from Ibn 'Umar, Ibn Mas'ud, 'Ali, Ibn 'Abbas, Mujahid, Ka'b, ar-Rabi' and as-Suddi. Ibn Jarir at-Tabari relates them in his *Tafsir*, as do Ibn Mardawayh, al-Hakim, Ibn al-Mundhir, Ibn Abi Dunya, al-Bayhaqi, and al-Khatib in their *tafsirs* and books."

The basic picture gained from these accounts is that when people among the descendants of Adam fell into acts of disobedience and disbelief in Allah, the angels in heaven said, "O Lord. You created this world for people to worship You and obey You and now they have committed acts of disobedience and rebellion and taken lives which they had no right to take, consumed property unlawfully, stolen, committed fornication and drunk wine." They began to curse them and did not find any excuse for them. It was said to them, "They are unaware," but they still did not excuse them.

One of the transmissions says that Allah said to them, "If you had been in their place, you would have done the same as them." They said, "Glory be to You! That would not be something we would do." Another transmission has, "They said, 'No.'" It was said to them, "Choose two angels from among yourselves whom I will command and forbid to disobey Me."

They chose Harut and Marut, who went down to earth and appetites were created in them. They were commanded to worship Allah and not to associate anything with Him and they were forbidden to take life without legal right to do so, and to consume unlawful property, steal, commit fornication or drink wine. They

38

remained in that way on earth for a considerable time, judging people by the Truth.

During that time, there was a woman whose beauty among people was like that of Venus among the stars. The two angels tried to seduce her but she refused unless they would submit to her authority and her religion. They asked her about her religion and she produced an idol for them. They said, "We cannot worship this," and they left and worshipped as Allah wished.

Then they came to her again and spoke humbly to her and tried once more to seduce her. Again she refused unless they took on her religion and worshipped the idol which she worshipped. They refused, and when she saw that they refused to worship her idol, she said to them, "Choose one of three things - either worship this idol, kill someone, or drink this wine.' They said, "None of them is good but the least bad of the three is drinking the wine." So she gave them wine to drink until they were completely under its influence. A man passed by while they were doing this and they were afraid that he would give them away so they killed him.

When the state of intoxication left them, they realised what a terrible mistake they had made and tried to ascend back up to heaven but they were unable to do so. Then the veil between them and the inhabitants of the heavens was removed. The angels looked at the wrong actions they had done and realised that those who are unaware are lacking in fear. After that they began to ask forgiveness for the people of the earth.

After they had committed this error, the two angels were told to choose between the punishment of this world and the punishment of the Next. They said, "The punishment of this world comes to an end, whereas the punishment of the Next world lasts forever." So they chose the punishment of this world and they were sent to Babel where they were punished by being suspended upside down by their feet.

In one transmission, it says that they taught the woman the word by which she could ascend to heaven and she ascended and Allah transformed her and she became the star known as Venus!

All this is part of the myths and lies of the tribe of Israel and is not corroborated either by intellect or transmission or *Shari'a*.

Some of the transmitters of this false fiction even go so far as to ascribe its transmission to some of the Companions and Followers but in doing so they enter the arena of sin and shameful crime and at the same time connect this lie to the Prophet, may Allah bless him and grant him peace, by taking it back to him. Glory be to You, my Lord, above and beyond this terrible lie!

Imam Abu'l-Faraj ibn al-Jawzi gave a judgement about this story, and ash-Shihab al-'Iraqi writes that anyone who believes that Harut and Marut were two angels who are being punished for their sin has disbelieved in Allah Almighty.

Qadi 'Iyad said in *ash-Shifa'*, "What is said in the reports and commentaries about the story of Harut and Marut does not relate anything, either sound or weak, from the Messenger of Allah, may Allah bless him and grant him peace, himself, and there is nothing which is taken by analogy." A similar judgement was made by Ibn Kathir in respect of tracing the material in this story back to the Prophet.

As for what does not go back to the Prophet, it is clear that it originates in the transmissions of the Jewish material taken from Ka'b and others. It is the heretics of the People of the Book who connected them to Islam. Thus accurate commentators, who are skilful in recognising the sources of the *deen,* refute them. Their intellects refuse to accept these myths, as do those of others such as Imam ar-Razi, Abu Hayyan, Abu's-Su'ud, al-Alusi, and others.

Furthermore, even from a rational point of view these transmissions are unsound. The angels are protected from all wrong action let alone these things which would not even issue from an evil human being. Allah informs us that the angels "do not disobey Allah in anything He commands them and they do everything they are commanded to," as is related in some transmissions which I indicated previously and in the words of Allah Himself.

Another of these transmissions has Allah saying to them, "If I tested you in the same way I tested the tribe of Adam, you would also disobey Me." They said, "If You were to do that, O Lord, we would certainly not disobey You!" To refute the words of Allah constitutes disbelief. Any human being who possesses knowledge of Allah and His attributes is free of that, let alone the angels. And how could a corrupt woman ascend to heaven and become a radiant star! What is that star which they claim to be Venus and at the same time a woman? She would have had to have been transformed on the day Allah created the heavens and the earth!

These myths are not corroborated either by sound transmission or sound reason. Not only that but they differ from what has become clear certainty through the knowledge of modern scientists. I do not understand what our position is supposed to be in respect of the astronomers and cosmologists since we do not repudiate these myths and are either silent about them or support them!

The true interpretation of the *ayat* mentioning this story

My concern in this book is not only to completely destroy and nullify these Israeli tales and myths, but also to explain these words, which have been twisted from their correct meaning, in a sound and scientific way corroborated by sound transmission and sound reason, and also the foregoing and subsequent passages, so that the reader will be increased in certainty. Allah says:

"*They follow what the shaytans recited during the reign of Sulayman. Sulayman did not reject but the shaytans did reject and taught people sorcery and what had been sent down to the two angels in Babylon, Harut and Marut. They taught no one until they had told him, 'We are merely a trial and a temptation, so do not reject.' From the two of them people learned how to separate a man from his wife. They do not harm anyone by it, except with the permission of Allah. They have learned what will harm them and bring them no benefit. They know that anyone who deals in it will have no share in the Next World. How evil the thing for which they have sold themselves if they only knew.*" (2:102)

There is nothing in this noble *ayat* which gives any indication whatsoever of this disreputable story. That was not the reason for the sending down of the *ayat*. The reason was that the shaytans in that distant time used to eavesdrop in the heavens and then add lies to what they had heard, which they would then pass on to the soothsayers and rabbis of the Jews. They, in turn, would record these fabrications in the books they read and taught to other people.

This spread in the time of Sulayman, peace be upon him, to the point that people said, "This is the science of Sulayman, and the kingdom of Sulayman was only made possible by it. It was by this means that he subjugated men and jinn and the wind which ran at his command." This is one of the lies the Jews told about the Prophets. Allah accused them of lying when He says, *"Sulayman did not reject but the shaytans did reject and taught people sorcery."*

Then He adds to that, *"and what had been sent down to the two angels in Babylon, Harut and Marut."* By *"what had been sent down"* He means the science of magic, which was sent down so that they could teach it to people and warn them against it. The reason the two of them were sent down was to teach people what magic was so that they would then know the difference between magic and prophethood, and therefore that Sulayman was not a magician. It was to ensure a complete understanding.

They did not, in any case, teach anyone magic until they had first cautioned him saying to him, "We are merely a temptation and a trial and a test, so do not become unbelievers by teaching it and using it." Part of the point of the teaching was to warn people against it and to teach them the difference between it and prophethood and prophetic miracles. There is nothing wrong with this. Indeed, it something desirable and meritorious if there is a real need for it.

However, people did not take their advice and they would use magic to separate a man from his wife. That was by the permission and will of Allah. The *ayat* indicates that it is permitted to teach people magic in order to warn people against succumbing to it and acting by it and there is no sin in that. It is also permissible to teach it to eliminate any resemblance between it and true miracles and prophethood and there is no sin in that. What is unlawful and a sin is to teach it or learn it in order to use it. This point is well illustrated by the sayings: "I learned evil not for evil's sake, but in order to be safe from it." And also: "People who do not recognise evil, fall into it."

When the Messenger of Allah, may Allah bless him and grant him peace, came to the Jews - may the curse of Allah be on them - they knew that he was the Prophet, the good news of whom had been given in the Torah, and they used to pray for his help against the idolworshippers before he was born and sent. But then when he did come to them, they would not acknowledge him and rejected him. They cast their book, the Torah, and the Book of Allah, the Qur'an, behind their backs.

Allah indicates that they should follow the clear truth but they preferred to follow the magic they had inherited from their fathers and which the shaytans had taught them, even though it was obligatory for them to reject magic and caution people against its evil. That was what the two angels, Harut and Marut, did: warn people against the evils of magic and against using it.

This is the sound *tafsir* of the noble *ayat*, not what stupid falsifiers claim. Through this understanding, harmony between the passages is obtained and the true value of the *ayat* is realised. I cannot imagine how people can see any connection between the Jewish material they have related and the words of the Almighty, *"They taught no one until they had told him, 'We are merely a trial and a temptation, so do not reject.'"* The extraordinary thing is that Imam Ibn Jarir talked about these things in his commentary of the *ayat* and apparently had no hesitation in doing so.

To summarise: the reader must be on guard against this Jewish material wherever it is used, whether in books of *tafsir, hadith*, history, admonitions or any other kind of literature.

Jibril: the Envoy to the Prophets

There are several accounts of the way the revelation started to come to the Messenger of Allah, may Allah bless him and grant him peace. Muslim transmitted in his *Sahih* from Ibn Shihab az-Zuhri who said that 'Urwa b. az-Zubayr had related to him that 'A'isha, the wife of the Prophet, may Allah bless him and grant him peace, said:

"The beginnings of revelation to the Messenger of Allah, may Allah bless him and grant him peace, took the form of true dreams. Whenever he had this kind of dream, it was something clear like the break of day. Then he was made to love going into retreat and used to retire to the cave of Hira' where he would devote himself to the worship of Allah alone, continuing in this worship for a number of nights until he felt inclined to return to his family. He would take provisions for his stay. Then he would return to Khadija to restock with provisions and do the same again. This lasted until the Truth came to him while he was in the cave of Hira. The angel came to him and said, 'Read!' He said, 'I cannot read.' The Prophet, may Allah bless him and grant him peace, said, 'He seized me and squeezed me until all the strength went out of me and then released me and said, "Read!" I said, "I cannot read."'

"'Then he seized me and squeezed me a second time until all the strength went out of me and then released me. Then he seized me and squeezed me a third time and then released me, and then he said, *"Read in the name of your Lord who created man from a blood clot. Read, and your Lord is the Most Generous."'*"

44

[She went on,] "Then the Messenger of Allah, may Allah bless him and grant him peace, returned with that, his heart quaking. He came to Khadija and said, 'Wrap me up! Wrap me up!' They wrapped him up until the state of terror had left him and then he said to Khadija, 'O Khadija, what is wrong with me!' and told Khadija what had happened and said, 'I am afraid for myself.' Khadija said to him, 'No, by Allah, Allah would never bring disgrace upon you. You maintain ties of kinship, speak the truth, bear people's burdens, help the destitute, give hospitality to your guests and help those who have been afflicted by calamities.'

"Khadija then went with him to her cousin, Waraqa ibn Nawfal ibn Asad ibn 'Abdu'l-'Uzza, who had become Christian during the *Jahiliyya*. He could write Hebrew and had written in it as much of the Evangel as Allah willed. He was an old man who had gone blind. Khadija said, 'Cousin! Listen to your nephew.' Waraqa said to him, 'Nephew, what is it that you have seen?' The Messenger of Allah, may Allah bless him and grant him peace, told him what he had seen. Waraqa said to him, 'This is the *Namus* which was sent to Musa, may Allah bless him and grant him peace. I wish that I were still young. I hope I will still be alive when your people drive you out!' The Messenger of Allah, may Allah bless him and grant him peace, said, 'Will they drive me out?' He said, 'Yes, no man has brought anything similar to what you have brought without being treated with hostility. If I am still alive on that day, I will give you my strong support.'"

The words, "This is the *Namus* which was sent to Musa," refer to Jibril, may Allah bless him and grant him peace. The people of language and rare *hadith* say that linguistically the "*namus*" is someone with a good secret and the "*jasus*" is someone with an evil secret. Scholars agree that Jibril, peace be upon him, is called the *Namus* and they agree that he is what is meant here. Imam al-

Hurawi said, "He is called that because Allah Almighty singled him out for the unseen and revelation."

Al-Bukhari transmitted with an *isnad* from Jabir b. 'Abdullah, in the *hadith* speaking about the time when there was a interval in the Revelation, that the Prophet, may Allah bless him and grant him peace, said:

> "While I was out walking, I suddenly heard a voice from heaven. I raised my eyes and there was the same angel who had come to me at Hira'. He was sitting on a chair between heaven and earth. I was afraid of him and returned home and said, 'Wrap me up! Wrap me up!' Then Allah sent down, *'O you shrouded in your mantle, arise and warn'*.... up to *'and avoid uncleanliness.'* After that revelation became intensive and continuous."

Al-Bukhari transmitted in his *Sahih* from 'A'isha, *Umm al-Mu'minin*, may Allah be pleased with her, that al-Harith b. Hisham asked the Messenger of Allah, may Allah bless him and grant him peace, "Messenger of Allah! How does the revelation come to you?" The Messenger of Allah, may Allah bless him and grant him peace, said:

> "Sometimes it comes to me like the ringing of a bell - and this is the hardest on me - which then leaves me after I have fully understood and retained what was said. Sometimes the angel comes to me in the form of a man and speaks to me and I retain what he says."

'A'isha, may Allah be pleased with her, said:

> "I saw him when the revelation was descending on him on a very cold day and when it left him his brow was dripping with perspiration."

Ibn al-Qayyim, may Allah have mercy on him, said that there were seven ways in which revelation came.

1) The first was the true dream. This was the beginning of revelation to the Prophet, may Allah bless him and grant him peace. Whenever he had this kind of dream, it was clear like the break of day.

2) There was also what the angel imparted to his soul and heart without him seeing him, as the Prophet, may Allah bless him and grant him peace, said, "The Spirit of Purity imparted to my heart that no self dies until its provision is complete, so fear Allah and be moderate in asking. Do not let delay of provision move you to seek it by disobeying Allah. What is with Allah is only obtained by obeying Him."

3) The third was that the angel used to take on the form of a man for the Prophet, may Allah bless him and grant him peace, and speak to him so that he remembered what he said to him. It is in this form that the Companions used sometimes to see him.

4) Revelation used also to come to him like the ringing of a bell. This was the hardest for him. The angel would make it so difficult for him that his brow would drip with perspiration on even a very cold day and his camel would be forced into kneeling on the ground when he was riding it. On one occasion revelation came like that when his thigh was resting on the thigh of Zayd b. Thabit and it became so heavy that it nearly broke Zayd's thigh.

5) The fifth way was that he saw the angel in his true form and he would reveal to him whatever Allah wished to reveal to him. This occured twice to the Prophet, may Allah bless him and grant him peace, as Allah Almighty mentions in *Surat an-Najm*.

6) The sixth was when Allah revealed things to him directly such as the obligation of the prayer and other things when he was above the heavens during the Night Journey.

7) The seventh were the words of Allah which came to Him without the intermediary of the angel, in the same way that Allah spoke to Musa son of 'Imran. This kind of revelation is absolutely confirmed in the case of Musa by the text of the Qur'an and in the case of our Prophet, may Allah bless him and grant him peace, in the *hadith* of the Night Journey.

The Attributes of Jibril, the Trustee of the Revelation

The Almighty says:

"By the star when it plunges, your comrade is not astray nor does he err nor does he speak out of caprice. This is nothing but a revelation revealed, taught him by one terrible in power, endowed with strength, he stood poised..." (53:1-6)

And Allah Almighty says,

"Truly this is the word of a noble Messenger, having power, secure with the Lord of the Throne, obeyed, more-over trustworthy." (81:19-21)

Ibn al-Qayyim, may Allah have mercy on him, says of these *ayats*, "Allah, glory be to Him, has described His angelic messenger, Jibril, in this *sura* as being noble, strong, secure with his Lord, obeyed in the heavens, and trustworthy. These five qualities contain testimony of the trustworthiness of the *isnad* of the Qur'an and that Muhammad, may Allah bless him and grant him peace, heard it from Jibril, peace be upon him, and that Jibril heard it from the Lord of the worlds. This *isnad* should be enough for you in respect of sublimity and majesty.

"The first quality is that the Messenger who brought it to Muhammad, may Allah bless him and grant him peace, had 'nobility'. This refutes the words of his enemies about Shaytan being the one who brought it. Shaytan is foul and repulsive, vile, ugly and totally lacking in good. His inward is more ugly than his outward and his outward more evil than his inward. There is no good in him or with him. He is the furthest thing from nobility. The Messenger who brought the Qur'an to Muhammad, may Allah bless him and grant him peace, was noble and of beautiful appearance. Allah describes him in *Surat an-Najm*, as *"endowed with strength"*. Ibn 'Abbas said that this means to have a beautiful appearance and radiant form, to be full of excellence, good and wholesomeness, teaching those who are good. Every good in the earth is from guidance, knowledge, gnosis and belief and piety. That is part of what his Lord makes happen at his hand. This is the utmost degree of nobility in form and meaning.

"The second quality is "power", as Almighty says in *Surat an-Najm, "Taught by one terrible in power."* That calls our attention to several things. One of them is that by his strength he prevents shaytans from coming near him and obtaining anything from him and adding to or detracting from it. Rather, when Shaytan sees him, he flees from him and does not come near him. A second is that he is a supporter of the Messenger whom they denied and is his assistant, friend and helper. Whoever has this powerful one as his friend, helper, aide and teacher is the assisted guide and Allah is his guide and helper. Another is that anyone who opposes this Messenger also opposes his companion and friend, Jibril, and whoever opposes someone with power and force exposes himself to destruction. Yet another is that he is able to carry out what he is commanded to do on account of his power and is not incapable of doing it and conveying his trust as he was commanded. He is the Strong Trustee.

The third attribute is in the words of the Almighty, *"secure with the Lord of the Throne,"* i.e. he has position and standing with Him and is the nearest angel to Him. It is indicated by His words, *"with the Lord of the Throne,"* indicating the high position of Jibril, peace be upon him, since he was near to the Lord of the Throne - glory be to Him!

The fourth attribute is in His word, *"obeyed."* This makes it clear that his troops and helpers obey him when he delegates them to help his companion and friend, Muhammad, may Allah bless him and grant him peace. It contains an indication that Jibril is obeyed in the heavens and that both of the Messengers are obeyed in their respective places and by their people. It also shows esteem for him since he has the position of kings who are obeyed among their people. Allah did not appoint to this immense matter anyone other than someone who would be obeyed like a king.

The fifth attribute is in the words of the Almighty, *"then trust-worthy."* His being described with trustworthiness contains an indication of the careful preservation of what he carried and of the fact that he conveyed it properly.

The Enmity of the Jews to Jibril

At-Tirmidhi reports that the Jews said about the Prophet, may Allah bless him and grant him peace, "He is not one of the Prophets unless one of the angels comes to him from the presence of his Lord with the message and revelation. 'Who is your companion that we should follow you?'" He said, "Jibril." They said, "He is the one who brings down war and fighting. He is our enemy! If you had said Mika'il who brings down the rain and mercy, we would have followed you." So Allah sent down His words:

> *"Say, 'Anyone who is an enemy of Jibril - he was the one who brought it down upon your heart, by the authority of Allah, confirming what came before it, as guidance and good news for the believers. Anyone who is an enemy of Allah and His angels and His Messengers and Jibril and Mika'il, Allah is an enemy of the rejectors.'"* (2:97-98)

The Jews claim that Jibril, peace be upon him, was their enemy and that this enmity is what prevented them from believing in the prophethood of Muhammad, may Allah bless him and grant him peace, since the one who brought him the revelation was Jibril, peace be upon him. The truth is that their enmity to him stemmed from rancour and envy since they disliked the fact that prophethood had moved from them to this middle community and that Jibril, peace be upon him, had descended with the firm *deen* which abrogates all other *deens*.

Allah - glory be to Him! - made it clear that the affair was not Jibril's. Rather the affair was Allah's entirely. That is why Allah says, *"He was the one who brought it down upon your heart, by the authority of Allah."* i.e. Jibril the Trustee brought this Qur'an down on your heart, O Muhammad, by the command of Allah Almighty, *"confirming what came before it,"* of the divine books, and *"as guidance and good news for the believers,"* i.e. it contains perfect guidance and delightful good news of the Gardens of Bliss for the believers.

Al-Qurtubi said, "The *ayat* indicates the honour of Jibril, peace be upon him, and the censure of all who oppose him. The words of the Almighty, *"Anyone who is an enemy of Allah and His angels and His Messengers and Jibril and Mika'il, Allah is an enemy of the rejectors,"* is a threat and a rebuke to all opponents of Jibril, peace be upon him, and it informs us that enmity to some things necessarily entails Allah's enmity in return. The enmity of the slave in respect of Allah is to disobey Him and to avoid obeying Him, and to be hostile towards His friends. Allah's enmity to the slave is to punish him and to cause the effects of enmity to appear on him.

"If it is said: 'Why did Allah single out Jibril and Mika'il for mention, when the mention of the angels included them in any case?' the answer is that He singled out the mention of the two of them to honour them and also because the Jews had mentioned them in particular. They were therefore the direct cause of the *ayat* being sent down and it was necessary to mention them so that the Jews could not then say, 'We did not oppose Allah and all His angels.' Thus Allah mentioned them both to counter the interpretation that they might make."

The Night Journey of the Messenger of Allah to the Highest Heavens

Muslim transmitted in his *Sahih* from Anas b. Malik that the Messenger of Allah, may Allah bless him and grant him peace, said:

"Buraq was brought to me, a tall white animal some-what larger than a donkey but smaller than a mule. Its hoof alights at the point reached by its glance." He said, "I mounted and rode it until I reached Jerusalem." He said that he tied it to the ring to which the Prophets tie their mounts.

He said, "I entered the mosque and prayed two *rak'ats* in it. Then I left and Jibril, peace be upon him, brought me a cup of wine and a cup of milk. I chose the milk and Jibril said, 'You have chosen the natural way.'

"Then he took me up to the lowest heaven and Jibril asked for it to be opened. It was said, 'Who are you?' He said, 'Jibril.' It was said, 'Who is with you?' He said, 'Muhammad.' It was said, 'Has he been sent for?' He said, 'He has been sent for.' So it was opened for us and there I found Adam. He greeted me and prayed for good for me and then took us up to the second heaven and Jibril, peace be upon him, asked for it to be opened. It was said, 'Who are you?' He said, 'Jibril.' It was said, 'Who is with you?' He said, 'Muhammad.' It was said, 'Has he been sent for?' He said, 'He has been sent for.' So it was opened for us and I found there my cousins, 'Isa b. Maryam and Yahya b. Zakariyya, the blessings of Allah be upon them. They greeted me and prayed for good for me and then took me up to the third heaven and Jibril asked for it to be opened. It was said, 'Who are you?' He said, 'Jibril.' It was said, 'Who is with you?' He said, 'Muhammad, may Allah bless him and grant him peace.' It was said, 'Has he been sent for?' He said, 'He has been sent for.' So it was opened for us and I found there Yusuf, may Allah bless him and grant him peace. He was given half of all beauty and he greeted me and prayed for good for me and then he took us up to the fourth heaven. Jibril, peace be upon him, asked for it to be opened. It was said, 'Who are you?' He said, 'Jibril.' It was said, 'Who is with you?' He said, 'Muhammad, may Allah bless him and grant him peace.' It was said, 'Has he been sent for?' He said, 'He has been sent for.' So it was opened for us and I found there Idris. He greeted me and prayed for good for me. Allah, the Mighty and Majestic, says, *'We raised him up to a high place.'*

"Then he took us up to the fifth heaven. Jibril asked for it to be opened. It was said, 'Who are you?' He said, 'Jibril.' It was said, 'Who is with you?' He said, 'Muhammad.' It was said, 'Has he been sent for?' He said, 'He has been sent for.' So it was opened for us and I found there Harun, may Allah bless him and grant him peace. He greeted me and prayed for good for me. Then he took us up to the sixth heaven and Jibril, peace be upon him, asked for it to be opened. It was said, 'Who are you.?' He said, 'Jibril.' It was said, 'Who is with you?' He said, 'Muhammad.' It was said, 'Has he been sent for?' He said, 'He has been sent for.' So it was opened for us and I found there Musa, may Allah bless him and grant him peace. He greeted me and prayed for good for me.

"Then he took us up to the seventh heaven. Jibril asked for it to be opened. It was said, 'Who are you?' He said, 'Jibril.' It was said, 'Who is with you?' He said, 'Muhammad.' It was said, 'Has he been sent for?' He said, 'He has been sent for.' So it was opened for us and I found myself with Ibrahim, may Allah bless him and grant him peace, who was leaning with his back against the Frequented House. Every day 70,000 angels visit it, never returning to it again. Then he took me to the Lote Tree of the Furthest Limit whose leaves were like elephants' ears and fruits were like earthenware jugs."

He said, "When it was covered over by the command

of Allah, a change came over it and nothing in Allah's creation would be able to describe it owing to its extreme beauty. Allah revealed to me what He revealed and made fifty prayers obligatory for me in every day and night. Then I went down to Musa, may Allah bless him and grant him peace, who said, 'What did your Lord make obligatory for your community?' I said, 'Fifty prayers.' He said, 'Go back to your Lord and ask him to reduce it. Your community will never be able to do that. I know by my experience of the tribe of Israel.'"

He said, "I went back to my Lord and said, 'O Lord, reduce it for my community,' and he reduced it for me by five. I went back to Musa and said, 'He reduced it by five for me.' He said, 'Your community will not be able to do it. Go back to your Lord and ask him to reduce it.'"

He said, "I continued to go back and forth between my Lord, the Blessed and Exalted, and Musa, peace be upon him, until He said, 'O Muhammad, they are five prayers every day and night, but each prayer counts as ten so that makes fifty prayers. Whoever intends a good action and does not do it, a good action will be written down for him. If he does it, ten will be written down for him. Whoever intends an evil action and does not do it, nothing will be written against him. If he does it, one evil action will be written down.'"

He said, "I went back down to Musa, may Allah bless him and grant him peace, and informed him and he said, 'Go back to your Lord and ask him to reduce it.'" The Messenger of Allah, may Allah bless him and grant him peace, said, "I said, 'I have returned to my Lord so often that I am ashamed before Him.'"

An-Nawawi said in the commentary of this *hadith*, "The Qadi said that this *hadith* indicates that heaven has real gates with sentries guarding them, and it contains affirmation of the need to ask permission before entering."

An-Nawawi said, "As for the words of the sentries of heaven,

'Has he been sent for?' it means: 'Have you been sent to him to conduct him on the Night Journey and Ascent through the heavens.' It is not a question going back to the basis of the mission and the message."

The words of the Prophet, may Allah bless him and grant him peace, "Then he took me to the Lote Tree of the Furthest Limit," occurs sometimes with the definite article (as-Sidra al-Muntaha), and in some variants as Sidra al-Muntaha. Ibn 'Abbas and the commentators and others said that it is called the Lote tree of the Furthest Limit because the knowledge of the angels stops there and no one was able to go beyond it except the Messenger of Allah, may Allah bless him and grant him peace.

It is related from Ibn Mas'ud, may Allah be pleased with him, that it is called that because it is reached both by what comes down to it from above it and also by what comes up to it from underneath of the command of Allah Almighty.

Jibril teaching the Messenger of Allah Wudu' and the Prayer

Ahmad transmits in his Musnad and al-Hakam in his Mustadrak from Zayd b. Haritha that the Messenger, may Allah bless him and grant him peace, said:

> "Jibril came to me at the beginning of what he revealed to me and taught me how to do wudu' and the prayer...."

Al-Bukhari transmits that the Messenger, may Allah bless him and grant him peace, said:

> "Jibril descended and led me in the prayer and I prayed with him, then I prayed with him, then I prayed with him, then I prayed with him, and then I prayed with him," and he counted out five times on his fingers.

The Angels coining a metaphor for the Prophet

Al-Bukhari transmitted that Jabir b. 'Abdullah said, "The angels came to the Prophet, may Allah bless him and grant him peace, while he was asleep and some of them said, 'He is asleep,' while others said, 'The eye sleeps but the heart is awake.' They said, 'There is a metaphor suitable for this companion of yours.' One said, 'So coin a metaphor for him.' Some of them said, 'He is asleep' and others said, 'The eye sleeps but the heart is awake.' They said, 'His metaphor is that of a man who builds a house and lays out a feast in it and sends out a summoner to invite people to it. All who answer the summoner enter the house and partake of the feast. Those who do not answer the summoner, do not enter the house and do not partake of the feast.' They said, 'Interpret it for him so that he can understand it.' Some of them said, 'He is asleep.' and others said, 'The eye sleeps but the heart is awake.' They said, 'The house is the Garden and the caller is Muhammad, may Allah bless him and grant him peace. All who obey Muhammad, may Allah bless him and grant him peace, have obeyed Allah. Those who disobey Muhammad, may Allah bless him and grant him peace, have disobeyed Allah.'"

Jibril giving good news of the Garden to Khadija

Al-Bukhari transmitted that Abu Hurayra, may Allah be pleased with him, said, "Jibril came to the Prophet, may Allah bless him and grant him peace, and said:

'O Messenger of Allah, this is Khadija who is bringing with her a vessel containing condiments or food and drink. When she comes to you, greet her from her Lord and from me, and give her the good news of a house in the Garden made from a hollow pearl in which there will never be any shouting or tiredness.'"

56

At-Tabarani transmitted in *al-Awsat* from the *hadith* of Fatima, may Allah be pleased with her, who said, "I said 'Messenger of Allah, where is my mother, Khadija?' He said, 'In a house made of a hollow pearl.' I said,'Where is this pearl?' He said, 'It is not like the kind of pearls which are strung as pearls and rubies.'"

As-Suhayli said, "The purpose of using the word *qasab* for pearl and not the word *lu'lu'*, is that there is an aptness in the word *qasab* since she, may Allah be pleased with her, carried the day *'ahrazat qasab as-sabq'* by hastening to belief before anyone else."

He also said, "The mention of the house has a subtle meaning because she was the mistress of a house before the mission and then became the mistress of a house in Islam when there was no other house than hers, for there was no house of Islam on the face of the earth on the day when the Prophet, may Allah bless him and grant him peace, was first sent except her house. It is a virtue which no one but she shares." Ibn Hajar said, "There is another meaning in the mention of the house because the people of the Hosue of the Prophet, may Allah bless him and grant him peace, derive from it."

In the words, "any shouting or tiredness," *sakhab* means shouting and argumentation in which voices are raised, and *nasab* means exhaustion. As-Suhayli said that these two qualities, i.e. argumentation and fatigue, are apt because when the Prophet, may Allah bless him and grant him peace, called people to Islam, Khadija, may Allah be pleased with her, answered him willingly and did not make him need to raise his voice nor quarrel nor tire in doing it. On the contrary she removed every fatigue from him and comforted him in every desolation and made every difficulty easy for him. Therefore it is fitting that the place which she was given the good news of by her Lord should have attributes corresponding to her actions.

After his words, "Greet her from her Lord and from me," at-Tabarani adds in this transmision that she said "He is Peace and Peace is from Him and peace be upon Jibril." In the variant of an-Nasa'i, she said, "Allah is Peace, and peace be upon Jibril and on you, O Messenger of Allah, be the peace and mercy of Allah and

His blessings."

Scholars say that this story contains an indication of Khadija's superior understanding because she did not say, "And upon you be peace," as was the case with some of the Companions when they used to say in the *tashahhud*, "Peace be upon Allah." The Prophet, may Allah bless him and grant him peace, forbade them saying, "Allah is Peace, so say: 'Greetings belong to Allah.'" Thus Khadija, by the soundness of her understanding, knew that Allah does not have the word "peace" in the reply to Him as creatures do because Peace (*Salam*) is one of the names of Allah, and he also is called *Salama*, and neither of them are correct to use in replying to Allah.

Jibril leading the Angels in the Battle of Badr

Allah says:

> "*Allah helped you at Badr when you were in a pitiful state, therefore be fearful of Allah, so that hopefully you might be thankful. When you said to the believers, 'Is it not enough for you that your Lord reinforced you with three thousand angels sent down?' No indeed! If you are steadfast and Godfearing and this time they come upon you suddenly, your Lord will reinforce you with five thousand angels, clearly-marked. Allah only did this to be good news for you and so that your hearts would be made tranquil by it. Victory comes from none but Allah, the Mighty, the Wise.*" (3:123-126)

And He says in *Surat al-Anfal:*

> "*When your Lord was revealing to the angels, 'I am with you so make those who believe firm. I will cast terror into the hearts of those who reject, so strike their necks and strike every finger of them!'*" (8:12)

The angels are the troops of Allah. He strikes with them any of

His slaves He wishes. Allah Almighty informs us that He helped the Muslims in the Battle of Badr by means of the angels in answer to their call for help and to strengthen them with the support and feeling of tranquillity that the angels cast into their hearts.

Ar-Rabi' b. Anas said, "Allah helped the Muslims with a thousand and then they became 3000 and then 5000."

Al-Bukhari says in his *Sahih* in the "Chapter of the Presence of the Angels at Badr" from Mu'adh b. Rifa'a b. Rafi' az-Zurqi from his father who was one of the people of Badr. He said, "Jibril came to the Prophet, may Allah bless him and grant him peace, and said, 'How do you gauge the people of Badr among you?' He said, 'Among the best of the Muslims.' He said, 'It is the same with those of the angels who were present at Badr.'"

Ar-Rabi' b. Anas said, "On the day of Badr people could see those who had been slain by the angels among the dead by the blows above the necks and on their fingertips which looked as if fire had burnt them." (Al-Bayhaqi transmitted it.)

Al-Qurtubi said, "The descent of the angels is one of the means of achieving victory which is in itself not necessary for the Almighty Lord but which His creatures do need. Therefore the heart should be connected to Allah and trust in Him, for He is the One who helps both through means and also without means. *"His command when He desires something is but to say to it, 'Be!' and it is."* (36:81) But He informed us about that so that creation would take note of the means which existed in the past which they were commanded to observe. *"You will not find any changing in the practice of Allah."* (33:62) That does not diminish trust in Allah in any way and it refutes those who say that means are only for the weak, not the strong. The Prophet, may Allah bless him and grant him peace, and his Companions were the strong and other people are the weak. This is clear."

The Angels helping in the Battle of the Confederates

The Almighty says:

"O you who believe! Remember Allah's blessing to you

59

when forces came against you and We sent against them a
wind and other forces that you could not see. Allah sees
everything that you do..." (33:9)

Ibn Kathir says that the Almighty reports about His blessing, bounty and goodness to His believing slaves in averting their enemies and defeating them in the year in which they joined forces and allied themselves against them. That is referring to the Affair of the Ditch which took place in Shawwal, 5 AH, according to most well-known sources.

Musa b. 'Uqba and others said that it happened in 4 AH, and that the reason the Confederates came was that a group of the Jewish nobles of Banu'n-Nadir, who had been exiled from Madina by the Messenger of Allah, may Allah bless him and grant him peace, to Khaybar, including Sallam b. Abi'l-Huqayq, Huyayy b. Akhtab and Kinana b. Abi'l-Huqayq, went to Makka and met with the nobles of Quraysh and encouraged them to fight the Prophet, may Allah bless him and grant him peace, promising them their help and support. They agreed to do it.

Then they went out to the tribe of Ghatafan and invited them, and they also agreed. Quraysh went out with their battalions following them led by Abu Sufyan Sakhr b. Harb. In charge of Ghatafan was 'Uyayna b. Hisn b. Hudhayfa. Altogether they numbered about 10,000 men.

When the Messenger of Allah, may Allah bless him and grant him peace, learned of their advance, he commanded the Muslims to dig a ditch around Madina on the eastern side. That was on the suggestion of Salman al-Farisi, may Allah be pleased with him. So the Muslims worked on it, putting much effort into it and the Messenger of Allah shifted the earth and dug with them.

The idolworshippers came and camped on the eastern side of the city near Uhud and another group of them camped in the upper part of Madina as the Almighty says, *"When they came at you from above you and below you."* The Messenger of Allah, may Allah bless him and grant him peace, and the Muslims with him came out. There were about 3000 of them, though some say 7000. They had their backs to Sal' and their faces towards the enemy.

The ditch had been dug, but there was no water in it to stop the horses and men from reaching them. He kept the women and children inside the fortresses of Madina.

The Banu Qurayza were a tribe of Jews who had a fortress to the east of Madina and they had a treaty with the Prophet. They had about 800 fighters. Huyayy of the Banu Nadir went to them and kept at them until they broke their treaty and supported the confederates against the Messenger of Allah. Thus the danger was great, the business very grave and the situation dire as Allah Almighty says, *"At that time the believers were tested and severely shaken."*

They continued to besiege the Prophet, may Allah bless him and grant him peace, and his Companions for about a month although they did not attack them and there was no fighting between them except when 'Amr b. 'Abdu Wudd al-'Amiri, one of the bold horsemen famous in the *Jahiliyya,* rode forward with some horsemen and crossed the ditch, reaching part of the Muslims. The Messenger of Allah detailed some riders of the Muslims to meet him. It is also said that no one went out to him. He commanded 'Ali, may Allah be pleased with him, to go out to him and they fought for some time and then 'Ali killed him. That was a sign of impending victory,

Then Allah Almighty sent a strong wind against the Confederates which blew so fiercely that they had no tents left standing nor could they light a fire nor would anything stay in its place. So they they left in disappointment and loss as the Almighty says:

"O you who believe! Remember Allah's blessing to you when forces came against you and We sent against them a wind and other forces that you could not see."

Ibn Kathir says that His words, *"other forces you could not see"*, mean the angels who unsettled them and cast terror and fear into their hearts. The leader of every tribe said "O Banu so-and-so! To me!" and they gathered to him and he was saying, "Help! Help!" when Allah Almighty cast terror in their hearts.

The Angels Helping the Messenger of Allah against the Jews

As has already been mentioned, when the armies of the Confederates came and camped at Madina, the Banu Qurayza broke the treaty they had concluded between themselves and the Messenger of Allah. When news of that reached the Messenger of Allah, may Allah bless him and grant him peace, it greatly upset him and was very hard on him and the Muslims. When Allah helped him and the enemy forces retreated and went back disappointed and empty-handed, the Messenger of Allah returned to Madina victorious and people laid down their weapons.

While the Messenger of Allah was washing off the dust of the expedition in the house of Umm Salama, may Allah be pleased with her, Jibril, peace be upon him, appeared to him with his brocade turban wrapped round the lower part of his face, riding on a mule on which there was a brocade saddle-cloth. He said, "Have you put down your weapons, Messenger of Allah?" He said, "Yes." He said, "But the angels have not put down theirs and will not return before seeking out the people. O Muhammad, Allah commands you to travel to the Banu Qurayza. I am going to them and will shake them." Muhammad ibn Ishaq related it.

Then al-Bukhari says from Anas b. Malik, may Allah be pleased with him, "It is as if I could see the dust rising in the alley of the Banu Ghanm from the procession of Jibril when the Messenger of Allah, may Allah bless him and grant him peace, went to Banu Qurayza."

Musa b. 'Uqba said in his *Raids* from az-Zuhri, "Jibril said to the Prophet, may Allah bless him and grant him peace, 'May Allah forgive you! Have you laid down your weapons?' He said, 'Yes.' Jibril said, 'We have not laid them down since the time the enemy first came upon you and I was seeking them out until Allah defeated them.' They say that traces of dust were on Jibril's face. Jibril said to him, 'Allah commands you to fight the Banu Qurayza and I am going to them with those of the angels who are with me to shake their fortresses, so bring out the people.'

"The Messenger of Allah, may Allah bless him and grant him peace, went out after Jibril and passed by a gathering of the Banu Ghanm who were waiting for the Messenger of Allah and he asked them, 'Did a horseman just ride past by you?' They replied, 'Dihya al-Kalbi passed by us on a white horse with a brocade cloth or rug under him wearing a bandage.' They mentioned that the Messenger of Allah, may Allah bless him and grant him peace, said, 'That was Jibril.' The Messenger of Allah, may Allah bless him and grant him peace, used to say that Dihya resembled Jibril."

The Angels in the Battle of Hunayn

Allah says:

"Allah has helped you on many occasions, and on the Day of Hunayn, when your great numbers delighted you but did not avail you in any way, and the earth seemed narrow to you for all its great breadth, and you turned your backs. Then Allah sent down His Tranquillity on His Messenger and on the believers, and sent down troops you did not see, and punished those who rejected. That is the repayment of the rejectors." (9:25-26)

Ibn Kathir said, "The Almighty mentioned to the believers His bounty to them and His goodness to them in helping them on many occasions in their expeditions with His Messenger and that their success was from Him and by His support and determination, not by reason of their great numbers. He informed them that help is from Him whether the group is few or many. On the day of Hunayn they admired their numbers but this did not help them in any way and they turned in retreat, all but a few of them who stayed with the Messenger of Allah, may Allah bless him and grant him peace. Then Allah's help and His support descended on His Messenger and on the believers who were with them to teach

63

them that victory is from the Almighty alone. Even if the group is small: *'how many a small force has triumphed over much greater numbers by the permission of Allah. Allah is with the steadfast.'* (2:249)"

An Extraordinary Dream

Al-Bukhari transmited from Samura b. Jundub, may Allah be pleased with him, who said:

"The Messenger of Allah, may Allah bless him and grant him peace, would often say to his Companions, 'Who among you had a dream last night?' Then anyone who Allah willed would recount his dream. One morning he said to us, 'During the night two men came to me and said to me, "Come on!" So I went with them. We came upon a man who was lying on his back while another man was standing over him with a stone which he dropped onto his head and crushed it. Then the stone rolled away from him and he went after the stone to retrieve it. When he returned to him, his head was whole again and had become as it had been in the first place. So he went back and hit him as he had done the first time. I said to them, "Glory be to Allah! Who are these two?"

"'They said, "Go on! Go on!" We went on and came to a man lying on his back and there was another man standing over him with an iron hook. He went to one side of his face and gashed open the side of his mouth until it reached the back of his neck and then his nostril to the back of his neck and his eye to the back of his neck. Then he moved to the other side and did the same thing as he had done to the first side. When he finished that side, the first side had become whole again. Then he did the same thing all over again." He said, "I said, "Glory be to Allah! Who are these two?"

"'They said to me, "Go on! Go on!" and we went on until we came upon something like an oven. In it was a babble and shouting. We looked down into it and it contained naked men and women. The flames leapt up at them from underneath, and when those flames reached them, they cried out. I said, "Who are they?"

"'They said, "Go on! Go on!" and we went on until we came to a river, red like blood. In the river there was a man swimming and on the bank of the river was a man who had many stones with him. When that swimmer swam and reached the one who had gathered the stones, he forced his mouth open and made him swallow a stone. Then he would begin to swim and would come back to him again. Whenever he came back to him, he forced open his mouth and made him swallow a stone. I said to them, "Who are these two?"

"'They said to me, "Go on! Go on!" and we went on until we came to a man with the most repulsive appearance you have ever seen. He was at a fire which he was kindling and which he was running around. I said to them, "Who is this?'

"'They said to me, "Go on! Go on!" and we went on until we came to a green meadow with every type of spring flower in it. There was, in the middle of the meadow, a man so tall that I could scarcely see his head, so high it was in the sky. Around the man were the greatest number of children I have ever seen. I said, "Who is this? Who are those?"

"'They said to me, "Go on! Go on!" and we went on until we reached a huge tree and I have never seen any tree bigger or more beautiful than it. They said to me, "Climb it." We climbed it and came to a city built of gold and silver bricks. We came to the door of the city and asked for it to be opened and it was opened for us and we entered it. We were met by men half of whose physique was the most beautiful you have ever seen and the other half was the ugliest you have ever seen. The two said to them, "Go and plunge into that river." There was a wide river flowing there whose water was pure white. They went and jumped into it and when they returned to us, that evil had left them and they had the most beautiful form.'

He said, 'They said to me, "This is the Garden of Eden, and that is your place." I raised my eyes upwards and there was a castle like a white cloud. They said to me, "This is your place." I said to them, "May Allah bless you, let me enter it." They said, "No, not now. But you will enter it."

"'I said to them, "This night I have seen marvels, but what are these things which I have seen?" They said to me, "We will tell you. The first man you came to whose head was being crushed with the stone is a man who memorised the Qur'an and the● abandoned it and slept through the obligatory prayers. As for the man you came to whose jaw was split to his neck, whose nostril to his neck and whose eye to his neck, he was a man who went from his house and told lies which spread everywhere. As for the naked men and women who were in something like an oven, they were adulterers and adultresses. The man you came to who was swimming in the river and being made to swallow stones used to consume usury. The man with the disagreeable appearance who was at the fire, kindling it and running around it, was Malik, the custodian of *Jahannam*. The tall man in the meadow was Ibrahim. The children who were around him are all those who were born and died in the natural state.'"

"Some of the Muslims asked, 'Messenger of Allah, the children of the idolworshippers as well?' The Mes-senger of Allah, may Allah bless him and grant him peace, said, 'The children of the idolworshippers as well. As for the people who were half beautiful and half ugly, they are the people who mixed righteous actions with evil actions. Allah pardoned them.'"

The meanings of the expressions in this *hadith* are explained in the *Fath al-Barr.* In his words, may Allah bless him and grant him peace, "During the night two men came to me," the two men are, as has come into another variant with Jarir b. Hazim, Jibril and Mika'il.

About his words, "They came to me," Ibn Jubayra says that it means they woke him up. It is possible that he saw in a dream that they woke him up and he saw what he saw in the dream and described it after he was awake, and his dream was like being awake. However what he was saw was a metaphor whose difficulty of interpretation indicated that it was a dream.

Regarding his words, "I went with them," Jarir adds in his variant "to the Holy Land", and with Ahmad we find, "to an open land". The *hadith* of 'Ali has, "They took me to heaven."

His words, "We came to a man who was lying on his back while another man was standing over him with a stone," means thrown onto his back. In 'Ali's *hadith* we find, "I passed by an angel in front of whom was a human being. The angel had a stone in his hand with which he was beating the human's head."

His word, "crushed it" means to shatter something hollow.

His words, "and the stone rolled away" means went from a high place to a lower one and it is the word used for something rolling down by itself.

His words, "When he returned to him, his head was whole again." Ahmad has here, "His head returned as it had been."

His words, "he gashed open the side of his mouth until it reached the back of his neck" means to split it in two. The *shidq* is the corner of the mouth. Ibn al-'Arabi said, "To gash open the corner of the mouth of the liar is to put the punishment in the site of the act of disobedience. It is on this basis that punishment occurs in the Next World, contrary to the way things happen in this world."

His words, "We came upon something like an oven," reads in the variant of Muhammad b. Ja'far. "Built like the structure of an oven," and Jarir adds, "Its top was narrow and its bottom wide, and there was a fire kindled under it."

His words, "they cried out" means they raised their voices in such a way that they were muddled up together.

His words, "which he was kindling" means setting fire to. It says in *at-Tahdhib*, "He kindled the fire with wood, he collected together for the fire scattered firewood. Ibn al-'Arabi says that it means poking the fire.

About the words, "we came to a green meadow", ad-Da'udi said that this refers to a meadow which is covered in green grass.

Instead of his words, "with every type of spring flower in it," another variant has, "all the flowers of spring."

His words, "plunge into that river" means to be immersed in it in order to wash away that attribute by this pure water.

His words, "that evil had left them" means the ugly side became the same as the beautiful side.

His words, "then abandoned it" is that abandoning the Qur'an after memorising it is a terrible crime because he imagines that he sees in it something that obliges him to abandon it. When he abandons the noblest of things, which is the Qur'an, he is punished in the noblest of limbs, which is the head.

His words, "and slept through the obligatory prayers" means that he was lazy about performing them in their correct times, and Allah has threatened those people in His words, *Woe to those that pray and are heedless in their prayers.*" (107:4-5)

His words, "they were adulterers" shows that nakedness is appropriate for them since they deserve to be disgraced because their custom was to conceal themselves in private. Therefore they are punished by exposure. The wisdom in bringing the punishment from underneath them is that their crime was from their lower limbs.

About his words "he used to consume usury," Ibn Hubayra said that the one who consumes usury is punished by swimming in the red river and being made to swallow stones because the basis of usury is to deal in gold and gold is red. As for the angel making him swallow stones, it indicates that nothing satisfied him. It is the same with usury. The one who uses it imagines that his wealth will increase but Allah wipes it out from behind him.

"The custodian of *Jahannam*" has a disagreeable appearance because that increases the punishment for the people of the Fire.

In the *hadith* of Abu Umama we find, "Then we went on and there were men and women of the ugliest appearance and the foulest smell, like that of sewers. I said, 'Who are these?' He said, there were corpses which were very swollen and had the foulest stench. I said, 'Who are these?' He said, 'Those are dead of the unbelievers.' Then we went on and there were some men asleep under the shadow of a tree. I said, 'Who are these?' He said, 'Those are the Muslim dead.' Then we went on and there were some men who had the handsomest faces and most fragrant perfume and I said, 'Who are these?' He said, 'Those are the truthful, the martyrs and the righteous.'"

Ibn Hajar said that this *hadith* contains many salutory lessons. Secrets make themselves known to people both in the waking and sleeping states in various ways. It also shows that some rebels are between the two worlds. There is the warning against sleeping through the prescribed prayers, against someone who has memorised Qur'an abandoning it, and against fornication, consuming usury and deliberately lying. It shows that those who have a palace in the Garden do not reside in it while in this world, but that happens after death, even in the case of Prophets and martyrs.

Their homes in the Garden are the highest homes, but that does not mean that they have a higher degree than Ibrahim, peace be upon him, since it is probable that he is residing in that place only on account of his tutelage of those children. His station is a station which is higher than that of the martyrs. This was already shown in the *hadith* of the Night Journey when the Prophet saw Adam in the lowest heaven. He was in that place in order to see the souls of his sons among the people of good and the people of evil, and to laugh or weep accordingly, although his station is in fact in 'Illiyin. On the Day of Rising, all people will be residing in their proper place and on that Day Allah will pardon all whose good and evil actions are equal in weight. O Allah! Pardon us by Your mercy, O most Merciful the merciful!

The *hadith* also shows the importance of dreams in general by the mere fact that the Prophet asked about them, the excellence of dream interpretation, and the preference for doing it after the *Subh* prayer because that is the time when the mind is most collected.

Righteous actions whose doers are prayed for by the Angels

Obedience to Allah Almighty on the Night of Power

The Noble Qur'an speaks of the descent of the angels to the earth on the Night of Power during the month of Ramadan. That is the night on which the Qur'an first came down to Muhammad, may Allah bless him and grant him peace, when the Qur'an descended from the Preserved Tablet down to the lowest heaven and heralded the descent of revelation on the Seal of the Prophets, may Allah bless him and grant him peace. This is why the angels descend during it, and Jibril the Trustworthy descends during it. He is the one meant by the word "Spirit" in Allah's words:

> *"On it the angels and the Spirit descend, by the leave of their Lord, upon every command. Peace it is, until the rising of dawn."* (97:4-5)

They do not descend on their own initiative, but only in obedience to divine authority, *"the leave of their Lord."*

Al-Qurtubi says in his *tafsir* of this noble *ayat*, *"On it the angels, and the Spirit descend, by the leave of their Lord, upon every command,"* i.e. they descend from every heaven and from the Lote Tree of the Furthest Limit and the dwelling-place of Jibril in the centre of it. They descend to the earth and give security to the people there making supplication until the moment of the rising of the dawn. That is the explanation of His words, *"On it the angels and the Spirit descend"*, i.e. Jibril, peace be upon him, *"by the leave of their Lord,"* at His command, *"upon every com-*

71

mand," i.e. every command which Allah decrees and decides from that year to the next. Ibn 'Abbas said that."

Anas said, "On the Night of Power, Jibril descends with a group of angels to pray and to greet every slave, standing or sitting, who is remembering Allah Almighty."

His words, *"Peace it is, until the rising of dawn"* mean that the Night of Power is peace and all good with no evil in it. *"Until the rising of dawn"* is until dawn breaks.

Ash-Sha'bi said, "It is the greeting of the angels to the people of the mosque from the time the sun disappears until dawn rises. They pass by every believer and say, 'Peace be upon you, O believer.'"

Recitation of Qur'an and *dhikr* of Allah Almighty

Al-Bukhari transmits with his *isnad* from Usayd b. Hudayr who said that once while he was reciting *Surat al-Baqara* at night, with his horse tethered beside him, it suddenly became very agitated. When he stopped reciting, the horse calmed down. When he started to recite again, the horse once more became agitated. Then he stopped reciting and the horse calmed down again. Then he recited and the horse became agitated so he stopped. His son Yahya was close to the horse and he was afraid that it might trample on him. When he pulled the boy away and looked up to the sky, he could not see it. In the morning, he told the Prophet, may Allah bless him and grant him peace, who said:

"Recite, Ibn Hudayr! Recite, Ibn Hudayr!" He said, "Messenger of Allah, I was afraid that the horse would trample on Yahya since he was near to it. I looked up and went to him. When I looked at the sky, there was something in it like a cloud containing something like lamps. So I left in order to not see it." He said, "Do you know what that was?" He said, "No." He said, "That was the angels who came near on account of your voice. If you had continued to recite, in the morning the people could

72

have looked at it and it would not have disappeared from them."

"The horse became agitated" means it jumped about. The words, "He pulled the boy away" means he dragged him from the place where he was fearing that the horse would trample on him. About the words, "He looked up to the sky, and he could not see it," Ibn Hajar says that this transmission is abridged. Abu 'Ubayd related it in full, saying, "He looked up to the sky and there was something in it like a cloud containing something like lamps. It rose up into the sky so that he could not see it."

The words of the Prophet, may Allah bless him and grant him peace, "Recite, Ibn Hudayr!" means that he should have continued reciting. It was not a command to recite at the moment of the conversation. It is as if the Prophet was visualising the situation and was present with him when he saw what he saw. It is as if he were saying: "Continue your recitation, so that the blessing continues with you by the descent of the angels and their listening to your recitation." So Usayd understood that and he replied giving an excuse for having curtailed his recitation, consisting of his words, "I was afraid it would trample on Yahya," i.e. I feared that if I continued reciting, the horse would trample on my son.

His words, "who came near" has, in the variant of Ibrahim b. Sa'd, the additional phrase, "to listen to you," and in the variant of Ibn Ka'b we find, "Usayd had a good voice." This addition indicates the reason why the angels were listening to his recitation.

An-Nawawi said, "This *hadith* shows that it is permissible for individuals of the community to see the angels." Ibn Hajar said, "This interpretation is sound, but it is limited, for instance, to the righteous, and to people with good voices."

He said that the *hadith* shows the excellence of recitation and the fact that it is a reason for the descent of mercy and the presence of angels.

Muslim transmits in his *Sahih* from Abu Hurayra, may Allah be pleased with him, who said that the Messenger of Allah, may Allah bless him and grant him peace, said:

73

"No people gather in any of the houses of Allah to recite the Book of Allah and to study it between them but that the *Sakina* descends on them and mercy covers them and the angels surround them and Allah remembers them to those in His presence."

In the two *Sahih* collections of al-Bukhari and Muslim. Abu Hurayra said that the Prophet, may Allah bless him and grant him peace, said:

"Allah, the Blessed and Exalted, has angels who travel the highways seeking out the people of *dhikr*. When they find people remembering Allah, the Mighty and Majestic, they call out to one another, 'Come to what you hunger for!' and they enfold them with their wings stretching up to the lowest heaven."

Ahmad transmitted in his *Musnad* as did Abu Ya'la al-Mawsuli and at-Tabarani in *al-Awsat* that Anas, may Allah be pleased with him, said that the Messenger of Allah, may Allah bless him and grant him peace, said:

"No people sit to remember Allah but that a caller from heaven calls out to them, 'Arise forgiven.'"

Muslim, at-Tirmidhi and an-Nasa'i transmit from the *hadith* of Mu'awiya:

"The Messenger of Allah, may Allah bless him and grant him peace, went out to a circle of his Companions and said, 'What is it that has caused you to sit together?' They said, 'We sat down to remember Allah and praise Him for He has guided us to Islam and been gracious to us.' He said, 'By Allah, is that the only thing that made you sit together?' They said, 'By Allah, we sat down for that reason alone.' He said, 'I did not make you swear out of any suspicion of you, but Jibril came to me and reported to me that Allah Almighty is boasting about you to the angels.'"

This boasting on the part of Allah Almighty is an indication of the nobility of *dhikr* in His sight and His love of it and that it has merit over other actions. *Dhikr* makes it mandatory for Allah Almighty and His angels to pray for those who do it. Whoever has Allah Almighty and His angels pray for him has complete success and total victory. Allah says:

> "O you who believe, remember Allah repeatedly. And glorify Him both morning and evening. It is He who calls down blessing on you, as do His angels, to bring you out of darkness into the light and, to the believers, He is most merciful." (33:41-43)

Ibn al-Qayyim said, "This prayer from the Almighty and His angels is the cause of people coming out the darkness to the light. When they receive the prayer from Allah Almighty and His angels and they are brought out of the darkness to the light, what good do they not obtain and what evil is not repelled from them! O alas for those who are heedless of their Lord! What blessing and bounty they are deprived of!"

Teaching people good

At-Tabarani and at-Tirmidhi transmitted with a sound *isnad* from Abu Umama that the Messenger of Allah, may Allah bless him and grant him peace, said:

> "Allah and His angels, and even the ant in its stone and the fish in the sea, pray for the one who teaches the people good." In another variant, "A man of knowledge has those in the heavens and the earth, even the fish in the sea, ask for his forgiveness."

75

Ibn Rajab al-Hanbali said, "Some scholars have mentioned that the secret of the animals of the earth asking for forgiveness for men of knowledge is that the men of knowledge command people to treat all creatures well and to kill those animals it is permitted to kill or slaughter properly. Therefore their good influence extends to all animals and that is why they ask forgiveness for them.

Another meaning is also evident from it, and that is that all animals obey Allah willingly, and glorify Him without disobeying. Therefore all creation which obeys Allah also loves the people who obey Him. So how much more so it is in the case of someone who truly knows Allah, His rights and the obedience due to Him! If anyone has this quality, Allah loves him and purifies him and praises him and commands His slaves among the people of the heavens and the earth and all creatures to love him and pray for him. That is their prayer on him, and He placed love for him in the hearts of His believing slaves."

The seeker of useful knowledge

Ahmad transmitted in his *Musnad* as did the people of the *Sunan* that Abu'd-Darda' said:

"I heard the Messenger of Allah, may Allah bless him and grant him peace, say, 'Allah will make the path to the Garden easy for anyone who travels a path in search of knowledge. Angels spread their wings for the seeker of knowledge out of pleasure for what he is doing. Everyone in the heavens and everyone in the earth asks forgiveness for a man of knowledge, even the fish in the water. The superiority of the man of knowledge to the man of worship is like the superiority of the moon to all the planets. The men of knowledge are the heirs of the Prophets. The Prophets bequeathe neither dinar nor dirham; they bequeathe knowledge. Whoever takes it has taken an ample portion.'"

Ibn Rajab said, "People disagree about the interpretation of the angels spreading their wings. Some of them apply its literal meaning, and say that what is meant is unfurling the wings and extending them to the seekers of knowledge in order to carry them on their wings to the places in the earth in which they are seeking knowledge, to help them in their quest and to make it easy for them. Some of them explain the spreading of the wings as meaning humility on their part and humbleness before the seeker of knowledge."

Ibn Rajab continued, "The meaning of the expression is open to question because the angels really have wings whereas humans do not. Some of them explain it as meaning the angels spreading their wings over the gatherings of *dhikr* up to the heaven as has come clearly in the *hadith* of Abu Hurayra. Something similar is related in some versions of the *marfu' hadith* of Safwan: 'The angels spread their wings over the seeker of knowledge and then one on top of the other until they reach the lowest heaven out of their love for what he seeks.' Perhaps this statement is the nearest to it, and Allah knows best."

Walking to the mosque and remaining in it

In the *Sahih* of Muslim we find:

"The angels pray on the one who comes to the mosque saying, 'O Allah, bless him! O Allah, show mercy to him! as long as he does no harm and does not break *wudu'*.'"

Abu Hurayra, may Allah be pleased with him, said that the Messenger of Allah, may Allah bless him and grant him peace, said:

"The group prayer is twenty-five degrees higher than the prayer in your house or the prayer in your place of business. Anyone who does *wudu'* and goes to the mosque with no other object than to do the prayer, Allah will raise him up a degree with every step he takes, and a wrong action will fall away from him. When he prays, the angels pray for him all the time he is in his place of prayer saying, 'O Allah! Forgive him! O Allah! Show mercy to him!' One of you is in the prayer as long as he is waiting for the prayer." In one variant, "'O Allah, forgive him! O Allah, turn to him as long as he does no harm in it and does not break *wudu'* in it.'"

Al-Bukhari, Muslim. Abu Dawud, at-Tirmidhi and Malik related it.

The meaning of "as long as he does no harm in it" is as long as he does not harm any of those praying by word or deed.

The meaning of "as long as he does break *wudu'*" is as long as no wind issues from him. This is why it recommended for a Muslim to do *wudu'* whenever he breaks it so that he obtains the prayer of the angels on himself.

Ibn Hajar said that this *hadith* demonstrates the virtues of the prayer over other actions by mentioning the prayer of the angels on him and their praying for mercy, forgiveness and *tawba* for him. It also demonstrates the excellence of the righteous people over the angels because they obtain degrees through their worship while the angels are occupied with asking forgiveness and supplication for them."

Praying in the first row

Abu Dawud and Ibn Majah and the *Musnad* of Ahmad all have that al-Bara', may Allah be pleased with him, said: "Allah and His angels pray on the first row."

In the *isnad* of at-Tirmidhi: "Allah and His angels pray on the front row."

Al-Bukhari transmitted that Abu Hurayra said that the Messenger of Allah, may Allah bless him and grant him peace, said:

"If people only knew what there was in doing *Dhuhr* at its time, they would race each other to it. And if they

78

knew what there was in the prayers of *'Isha'* and *Subh*, they would come to them even if they had to crawl. If they knew what there was in the call to prayer and the first row, they would draw lots for it."

Ibn Hajar said, "What is meant by the first row is the row immediately behind the Imam, and it is the first complete row behind the Imam, not one that has any gaps in it. Scholars say that this encouragement for people to join the first row is in order for them to hasten to discharge their responsibility, to hurry to enter the mosque, to be near the Imam and to listen to his recitation and learn from it and to be inspired by it and convey what he says, to be safe from someone else passing in front of him, to feel safe from seeing anyone in front of him, and for the place of his prostration to be safe from the coattails of anybody praying in front."

Going early to Jumu'a

In the *Sahih* of al-Bukhari, Abu Hurayra, may Allah be pleased with him, said that the Messenger of Allah, may Allah bless him and grant him peace, said:

> "On the Day of *Jumu'a*, the angels stand at the door of the mosque and write down the first to come and then those who follow. When the Imam comes out, they roll up their scrolls and listen to the reminder."

Ibn Hajar said in the *Fath* and Abu Nu'aym transmitted it as *marfu'* in *al-Hilya* with the expression, "On the Day of *Jumu'a*, Allah sends angels with scrolls of light and pens of light."

This indicates that the angels mentioned are not guardian angels. What is meant by the rolling up of the scrolls is to roll up the scrolls of the benefits connected with going early to Jumu'a as opposed to any other prayer; not those of listening to the *khutba*, catching the prayer, *dhikr*, supplication, humility and other such things. The guardian angels naturally write these things down. In the variant of Ibn 'Uyayna from az-Zuhri at the end of this *hadith* in Ibn Majah we find "Anyone coming after that, comes merely for the sake of the prayer."

The Fajr and 'Asr prayers in a group in the mosque

Abu Hurayra, may Allah be pleased with him, said that the Messenger of Allah, may Allah bless him and grant him peace, said:

"There are angels who take turns in being with you in the night and other angels in the day, and they meet together at the prayers of *Fajr* and *'Asr*. Then the ones who were with you during the night ascend and Allah asks them - although He knows better than they do - 'How were My slaves when you left them?' They say, 'When we left them they were praying and when we came to them, they were praying.'"

Al-Bukhari, Muslim, an-Nasa'i and Ibn Khuzayma related it.

About his words, "There are angels who take turns in being with you," Ibn Hajar said, "It is said that they are the guardian angels. Al-Qurtubi said, 'I think that the most evident view is that it is other than them. This view is strengthened by the fact that it is not transmitted that the guardian angels ever leave the slave nor that the guardian angels of the night are not the same as the guardian angels of the day.'"

'Iyad said, 'The wisdom of them meeting at these two prayers is part of Allah's kindness to His slaves and His generosity to them since He made the angels meet at a time when His slaves are in a state of obedience so that they can give the best testimony on their behalf."

Ibn Hajar said in the *Fath* ,"The *hadith* contains an indication of the immense importance of these two prayers since the two groups meet during them while there is only one group present

80

during the other prayers. This indicates the nobility of the two times mentioned. It is related that provision is allocated after the *Subh* prayer and that actions ascend at the end of the day. So whoever is engaged in an act of obedience at that time is blessed both in his provision and in his actions, and Allah knows best. It also shows that this community is honoured above others and means therefore that its Prophet is honoured above all other Prophets. It informs us of the love of Allah's angels for us so that our love for them is increased and we draw near to Allah by that. There are other salutory lessons, and Allah knows them best."

The meal of Sahur

Abu Sa'id al-Khudri said that the Messenger of Allah, may Allah bless him and grant him peace, said:

"*Sahur* is a meal containing blessing, so do not abandon it, even if you only have a drink of water. Allah and His angels pray on those who eat *sahur*."

Al-Mundhiri mentioned it in *at-Targhib wa't-Tarhib* from Ahmad, He said that its *isnad* is strong.

Ibn Hibban and at-Tabarani in his *Middle Collection* transmit from Ibn 'Umar, may Allah be pleased with him, that the Messenger of Allah, may Allah bless him and grant him peace, said:

"Allah and His angels pray on those who eat *sahur*."

Reliable people say that its *isnad* is good.

Sadaqa and spending in good ways

Al-Bukhari transmitted with his *isnad* from Abu Hurayra, may Allah be pleased with him, that the Prophet, may Allah bless him and grant him peace, said:

"There is no day which dawns on the slaves of Allah without two angels descending and one of them saying, 'O Allah, refund those who give money' and the other saying, 'O Allah, ruin those who withhold it.'"

There is also the *hadith* of Abu'd-Darda' who said that the Messenger of Allah, may Allah bless him and grant him peace, said:

"There is no day on which the sun rises but that it is accompanied by two angels who call out - and all of Allah's creation hear it except for men and jinn - 'O people! Hasten to your Lord. What is little and adequate is better than what is abundant and heedless.' And the sun does not set but that it is accompanied by two angels who call out and one of them says, 'O Allah, refund those who give money,' and the other, 'O Allah, ruin those who withhold it.'"

An-Nawawi says that praiseworthy spending is what is spent in acts of obedience and on behalf of your family and guests and in voluntary acts of charity. Al-Qurtubi said that this includes both obligatory and recommended giving, but that those who withhold from recommended giving do not merit this supplication nor those dominated by miserliness to the extent that they are not happy about giving out what is due from them, even if they do it.

The Hajj and standing at 'Arafa

At-Tabarani and others transmitted from the *hadith* of Abu Hurayra, may Allah be pleased with him, going back to the Prophet, may Allah bless him and grant him peace, who said:

When a man sets out for *hajj* with wholesome provision and places his foot in the stirrup and calls out, "At

Your service, O Allah,' then a caller from heaven calls out, 'At your service and obedience! Your provision is lawful and your mount is lawful and your *hajj* is accepted and unencumbered.' When a man sets out with unwholesome provision and puts his foot in the stirrup and says, "At Your service, O Allah,' then a caller from the heaven calls out, 'You have no service or obedience! Your provision is unlawful and your mount is unlawful, and your *hajj* is not accepted."

Muslim transmitted in his *Sahih* from 'A'isha, may Allah be pleased with her, that the Prophet, may Allah bless him and grant him peace, said:

"There is no day on which Allah more frequently frees His slaves from the Fire than the Day of 'Arafa and He draws near and boasts of them to the angels and asks, 'What do these people want?'"

From Jabir is that the Prophet, may Allah bless him and grant him peace, said:

"There is no day better with Allah than the day of 'Arafa. On it Allah, the Blessed and Almighty, descends to the lowest heaven to boast of the people of the earth to the people of heaven and He says, 'Look at My slaves, dishevelled, dusty, and without shade. They have come through every deep ravine, hoping for My mercy and they will not see My punishment.' So there is no day when more people are set free from the Fire than on the Day of 'Arafa."

Seeking martyrdom in the way of Allah

Jabir b. 'Abdullah, may Allah be pleased with both him and his father, said, "When my father was killed, I began to lift the cloth from his face, weeping, but they stopped me. The Prophet, may

Allah bless him and grant him peace, did not stop me. My aunt Fatima began to weep and the Prophet, may Allah bless him and grant him peace, said, "It does not matter whether you weep or do not weep. The angels were shading him with their wings until you removed it."

Al-Bukhari transmitted it and al-Bukhari has a chapter entitled, "The Chapter of the Angels shading the Martyr."

The prayer on the Prophet, may Allah bless him and grant him peace

Ahmad related in his *Musnad* and ad-Diya' in *al-Mukhtara* from 'Amir b. Rabi'a with a good *isnad* that the Messenger of Allah, may Allah bless him and grant him peace, said:

"There is no slave who prays for blessing on me but that the angels pray on him as long as he prays on me. So let the slave do a little or a lot of it."

Visiting the Sick

Ibn Hibban said in his *Sahih* with a sound *isnad* from 'Ali that the Messenger of Allah, may Allah bless him and grant him peace, said:

"No Muslim visits another Muslim without a thousand angels praying for blessings on him whatever hour of the day it is until evening, or whatever hour of the night it is until morning."

In a variant of at-Tirmidhi which an-Nawawi mentioned in the *Riyad as-Saliheen,* is that the Prophet said:

"No Muslim visits another Muslim without a thousand

angels praying blessing on him until the evening, or visits him in the evening without a thousand angels praying blessing on him until morning and he will have fruits in the Garden."

At-Tirmidhi said that its *isnad* is good.

Visiting Brothers

Muslim transmitted in his *Sahih* from Abu Hurayra that the Prophet, may Allah bless him and grant him peace said:

"A man visited a brother of his in another town and Allah assigned an angel to guard him on his way. When he came to him, the angel said, 'Where are you going?' He said, 'I am going to visit a brother of mine in that town.' He said, 'Do you have any property with him that you want to check on?' He said, 'No, it is only that I love him for the sake of Allah.' He said, 'I am the messenger of Allah to you to tell you that Allah loves you as you love this man for His sake.'"

"On his way" means on his road.
"To check on it" means to see to it and seek to put it in order.

Supplication for believers who are not present

Allah Almighty says:

"And as for those who came after them, they say, 'Our Lord, forgive us and our brothers who preceded us in belief, and do not put into our hearts any rancour towards those who believe. Our Lord, surely You are the All-Gentle, the All-Compassionate." (59:10)

Muslim transmitted from the *hadith* of Abu'd-Darda' that the

Prophet, may Allah bless him and grant him peace, said:

"A supplication which a Muslim man makes secretly for his brother is answered. At his head is a guardian angel. Whenever he makes supplication for good for his brother, the angel who guards him says, 'Amen, and the same for you.'"

Sleeping in a state of wudu'

'Umar, may Allah be pleased with him, said that the Messenger of Allah, may Allah bless him and grant him peace, said:

"Whoever spends the night in a state of purity, spends the night with an angel close to him. He does not wake up without the angel saying, 'O Allah, forgive Your slave so-and-so, He has spent the night in a state of purity.'"

Ibn Hibban related it in his *Sahih* and al-Mundhiri mentioned it in *at-Targhib wa't-Tarhib*.

"Close to him" means what is next to a person's body, be it a garment or anything else.

His words, "He spent the night in a state of purity" is a reason for forgiveness being asked for him. It is part of what the angel said.

Ibn 'Abbas, may Allah be pleased with both him and his father, said that the Messenger of Allah, may Allah bless him and grant him peace said:

"Purify these bodies of yours and Allah will purify you. There is no slave who spends the night in a state of purity but that an angel remains close to him. He does not pass an hour of the night without saying, 'O Allah, forgive Your slave. He spent the night in a state of purity.'"

At-Tabarani related it in *al-Awsat* and al-Mundhiri said that its *isnad* is good.

Actions whose doers are cursed by the Angels

The curse on the unbelievers

Allah Almighty says:

> "How can Allah guide a people who have rejected after their belief? They bore witness that the Messenger was true and that the Clear Signs had come to them. Allah does not guide wrongdoing people. Those, their repayment is that the curse of Allah is on them and of all the angels and the whole of mankind. They are under it forever. The punishment will not be lightened for them. They will be granted no reprieve." (3:86-88)

And He says:

> "Those who reject, and die while still rejectors, the curse of Allah is on them and of all the angels and the whole of mankind." (2:161)

The angels do not only curse the unbelievers but also those who commit the specific wrong actions listed below.

Preventing Allah's Shari'a from being implemented

In the *Sunan* of an-Nasa'i, Abu Dawud and Ibn Majah with a sound *isnad* from Ibn 'Abbas, may Allah be pleased with both him and his father, is that the Messenger of Allah, may Allah bless him and grant him peace, said:
"If anyone is murdered deliberately, someone should

be killed in retaliation for him. If anyone tries to prevent retaliation taking place, on him is the curse of Allah, the angels and all people."

Thus there is a curse on anyone who prevents the implementation of the judgement of Allah on someone who has murdered deliberately for the sake of rank or wealth. So how much more must this be the case when someone tries to prevent the implementation of the Shari'a as a whole!

Sheltering people of innovation

Among those Allah and the angels curse are those who innovate in the *deen* of Allah by abandoning its judgements and transgressing against its laws or sheltering and protecting people who do that, as has come in the sound *hadith:*

"Anyone who makes an innovation or shelters those who make innovations, on him is the curse of Allah, the angels and all people."

Abu Dawud, an-Nasa'i and al-Hakam transmitted it.

Abusing the Companions of the Messenger of Allah

In the collection of at-Tabarani, *al-Kabir,* from Ibn 'Abbas with a good *isnad* is that the Messenger, may Allah bless him and grant him peace, said:

"Anyone who abuses my Companions, on him is the curse of Allah, the angels and all people."

Women not responding to their husbands

Al-Bukhari transmitted with his *isnad* from Abu Hurayra, may Allah be pleased with him, that the Prophet, may Allah bless him and grant him peace said:

"When a woman spends the night spurning her husband's bed, the angels curse her until she returns." In another variant: "When a man calls his wife to bed and she refuses to come, the angels curse her until morning." In a third variant in the *Sahih* of al-Bukhari: "When a man calls his wife to bed and she does not come and he spends the night angry with her, the angels curse her until morning."

Ibn Hajar said in *al-Fath*, "About the words of the Prophet, 'She refuses to come,' Abu 'Awana adds in a variant, 'and he spends the night angry with her.' It is through this addition that the curse occurs because it is by that that her rebellion is confirmed, which is not the case when he is not angry about it. It might be that he excuses her or that he abandons his right. Censure is only directed against her when she is the one who spurns him and he is angry about it, or he spurns her because she is wrong-doing and does not renounce her wrong action. If he is the one who begins wrongly to spurn her, then it is another case."

He also said, "This *hadith* carries in it permission to curse a Muslim who is disobeying Allah if it is done in order to alarm him so that he will not engage in the action concerned. If he does engage in it, then you should ask for repentance and guidance for him. It shows that the angels continue cursing the people of disobedience as long as they are doing it. That, in turn, indicates that they also pray for the people of obedience as long as they are engaged in that. It also indicates that the angels' prayer for good or evil is accepted since he, may Allah bless him and grant him peace, was afraid of it.

"It guides women to helping their husbands and seeking to please them and it shows that men are less patient with regard to lack of sex than women, disclosing that the strongest cause of disturbance for a man is his impulse for lawful sexual intercourse. That is why the Lawgiver made it mandatory for women to help men in respect of it.

"It also goes to show that continuing to obey Allah and being steadfast in worshipping Him is in itself a reward for His slave since Allah did not omit any of his rights or fail to have them taken care of, to the extent that He has even made the angels curse someone who angers His slave by denying one of his appetites. In the same way it is therefore obligatory for the slave to fulfil the rights his Lord has over him."

A woman going out without her husband's permission

Ibn 'Umar, may Allah be pleased with both him and his father, said:

"I saw a woman who came to the Prophet, may Allah bless him and grant him peace, and said, 'Messenger of Allah, what rights does a husband have over his wife?' He said, 'His right over her is that she does not leave his house without his permission. If she does that, the angels of mercy and angels of anger curse her until she repents or returns.'"

The *hadith* is related by Abu Dawud, at-Tabalisi and al-Bazzar.

Someone pointing at his brother with a weapon

Muslim related in his *Sahih* that Abu Hurayra, may Allah be pleased with him, said that the Prophet, may Allah bless him and grant him peace said:

"If someone points with a piece of iron at his brother,

the angels curse him until he puts it down, even if it is his full brother."

Scholars say that the words of the Prophet, "the angels curse him" is to emphasise the general prohibition against anyone, whether he is hostile or not, whether in jest or in earnest, because to alarm a Muslim is absolutely unlawful. The curse of the angels on anyone who does it shows how unlawful it is.

Ibn al-'Arabi said, "If someone who merely points with a weapon deserves the curse, then what about someone who actually strikes with one? The pointer merits the curse, as has already been stated, whether his pointing is just a threat or whether it is in earnest or in jest. Even a joker is punished when he causes fear in his brother, and it is clear that the wrong action of a joker is less than that of someone who is serious."

The curse of the angels demonstrates the unlawfulness of this action which makes his brother alarmed and through which Shaytan might provoke him to kill his brother. This is particularly the case when the weapon concerned is one of these modern ones which can be discharged by the least error or unintentional touch. How many examples of this there are!

The Believer's Obligation towards the Angels

The angels are slaves of Allah whom He has selected and chosen and they have a high position with their Lord. The believer who worships Allah and seeks His pleasure must undertake to love and respect the angels and to avoid anything that might vex or harm them.

The things that distress them most are wrong actions, acts of disobedience, disbelief and associating others with Allah. Conversely what pleases the angels most is for a man's *deen* to be sincerely for his Lord and avoidance of all that angers Him.

That is why the angels do not enter places or houses in which Allah Almighty is disobeyed, or those in which there is something that Allah dislikes and hates, such as idols, images, and statues. Nor do they go near anyone who is involved in acts of disobedience to Allah such as drunkenness.

Abu Hamid al-Ghazzali said in his *Ihya'* that Abu Hurayra said, "The house in which the Qur'an is recited is spacious for the people in it and its good is abundant and the angels are present in it and the shaytans leave it. The house in which the Book of Allah, the Mighty and Exalted is not recited is narrow for the people in it and has little good and the angels leave it and the shaytans are present in it."

Al-Bukhari transmitted with his *isnad* from 'Ubaydullah b. 'Abdullah who heard Ibn 'Abbas, may Allah be pleased with both him and his father, say, "I heard Abu Talha say, 'I heard the Messenger of Allah, may Allah bless him and grant him peace, say, "The angels do not enter house in which there is a dog or an image."'"

Al-Bazzar related with a sound *isnad* from Burayda, may Allah be pleased with him, that the Messenger, may Allah bless him and grant him peace, said:

"There are three whom the angels do not go near: someone who is drunk, someone wearing saffron, and someone in *janaba*."

The angels are harmed by the same things that harm the sons of Adam, and this is confirmed in sound *hadiths*. They are harmed by foul smells, filth and dirt.

Al-Bukhari and Muslim related that the Messenger of Allah, may Allah bless him and grant him peace, said:

"Anyone who eats garlic and onions or leeks should not come near our mosque. The angels are harmed by what harms the sons of Adam."

Ibn Khuzayma and Ibn Hibban transmitted that Abu Ayyub said that the Messenger of Allah, may Allah bless him and grant him peace, was sent some food which consisted of vegetables and which contained onions or leeks. He did not see the Messenger of Allah, may Allah bless him and grant him peace, choose it, so he refused to eat as well. He said to him, "What is stopping you?" He said, "I did not see the trace of your hand." He said, "I am shy before the angels of Allah. It is not forbidden." In one variant we find, "Eat. I speak intimately with those with whom you do not speak intimately," i.e. the angels.

The Prohibition against Spitting to the right during the Prayer

The Messenger of Allah, may Allah bless him and grant him peace, forbade spitting to the right during the prayer because when a person stands in prayer, an angel stands on his right. In the *Sahih* of al-Bukhari from Abu Hurayra, may Prophet be pleased with him, is that the Prophet, may Allah bless him and grant him peace, said:

"When one of you stands for the prayer, he should not spit in front of him for he is speaking with Allah as long as he is in his prayer, nor to his right, for there is an angel on his right. He should spit to his left or under his foot and bury it."

In general, all believers should be godfearing, clean, penitent, regretful, full of remembrance and thankfulness so that they may have the company of the pious angels.

O Allah, take us back to You as Muslims and let us enter among Your righteous slaves by Your mercy!

Here ends this book. We ask Allah that everyone who reads it benefits from what is in it. Allah is the One who is asked for help.

The last of our words is: Praise be to Allah, the Lord of all the worlds.